STRAIGHT WIVES: SHATTERED LIVES

STORIES OF WOMEN WITH GAY HUSBAND

COMPILED AND EDITED BY
BONNIE KAYE, M.Ed.

ISBN: 978-1-60585-567-7

Dedication

This book is dedicated to the millions of straight women who struggle through years of their lives living a lie.

It is also dedicated to the late actress Vivien Leigh. We, as straight wives, share your pain and understand your heartache.

Front Cover an original work of art by M. Kathryn Massey
www.masseyfineart.com

Back cover an original work of art by Jean Lazar
"THEIR LAST PAINTING, Stories of Life That Will Rock Your Heart" by Jean Lazar can be purchased at www.authorhouse.com.

Introduction

My name is Bonnie Kaye. Since 1984, I have been counseling straight women who learn they are married to homosexual men. I have had the opportunity to help over 30,000 women through the years who thought they were at the end of the road of sanity. These were wonderful women who sacrificed years of their lives living in unfulfilling and often abusive marriages and never had a clue about the real issues. They entered the marriage with the same hopes, dreams, and expectations that all couples in love believe in. The disillusionment starts at different points for different women, but in the end, the impact is the same.

Women married to gay men feel extremely isolated and alone. They are embarrassed by their situation and sometimes believe they are at fault for their husbands' homosexuality. As the years wear on, the sense of self and sexual esteem is peeled away, one layer at a time. It has been my personal mission to help restore what has been taken away and destroyed. There is life after the death of these marriages when women are able to recover, heal, accept, and start over. Some of our women find true happiness with their new "soulmate," and some find a high level of happiness being on their own because they learn to love themselves first and foremost.

When I started counseling in this field after the demise of my own marriage to a gay man, I was uncertain as to the direction I would move in. I kept an open mind, trying not to be judgmental with women who were trying to find ways to cope in this situation that I call a mismarriage—meaning a mistaken marriage. Having just completed graduate school, I tried to follow the lessons learned throughout my counseling training— *allow women to draw their own conclusions and make their own decisions Encourage them to find their own answers and solutions.* In other words, if they decided they wanted to stay in their marriage, let them. And at first, I did.

After two years, I stopped. It didn't make sense. Why did women have to spend years struggling to change something that couldn't be changed? I threw out my textbook mindset and started to create my own philosophies based on what made sense to me. Those people who stayed together in marriages didn't seem any happier as the years went on. They struggled daily with insecurities, distrust, lack of sexual esteem, and poor self-image.

What I found interesting was in the marriages that stayed together, the men *didn't* change—at least not for the better. But the women *did* change. They lost sense of the person they were prior to the marriage. They became strangers to themselves and others. Many loaded up on medications to numb their brains so they wouldn't have to think. They became new age Stepford Wives—acting mechanically almost like programmed robots. Oh, some women tell me they call this "coping."

Coping is not living. It is existing, and that means being robbed of what you are entitled to in life. Yes, I say entitled because I believe that happiness is a given right of all people. They say that no one can make you happy, which is true. However, people can take away your happiness even if you have found it.

In 2000, my first book, "Is He Straight? A Checklist for Women Who Wonder" was published. To date, thousands of women have told me how this book has affected and changed their thinking and their lives. My second book, "Straight Wives/Gay Husbands: A Mutation of Life" in 2003 which was reprinted and added to and renamed "Doomed Grooms: Gay Husbands of Straight Wives" in 2004 followed up as the next step when women were able to accept their husbands' homosexuality and taught them how to move on. Although these books are both eye-opening and validating, this book, "Straight Wives: Shattered Lives" takes this subject to a whole new level. These are the stories of 27 women who share their lives with you.

The women who write in this book are members of my support network. They have been brave and generous enough to write and share their stories with the world to let people know of the hardships we endure as straight wives. They come from all over the country, and all over the world including India, the United Kingdom, and Australia. They are of different religions, cultures, and colors. They come from different social strata and economic situations. They have different educational levels and positions in life ranging from housewives to business owners and CEO's. What is so fascinating is that no matter what the situation is, the story line and the emotional hardship is the same.

If any woman who is reading this book is wondering what to do, I think by the end you will have your answers. You can read my closing comments at the end to help you make the most important life-saving decision of your life.

This book was initially inspired by the movie "Brokeback Mountain" which received tremendous international publicity in 2005. It tells the story of two mid-western men starting in the 1960's who fall in love and have an affair for several decades, but are stuck in the role of straight men due to the pressures that society placed on homosexuals in that time period. There was an outpour of public sympathy for the men whose lives were complicated by living lies throughout their marriages because of their inability to overcome the societal taboos of the day.

As women who lived this life, we were saddened and frustrated by the lack of depth portrayed by the wives in the movie. It seemed as if *our* part of the story was "skipped over" and ignored. After all, the movie was about the cowboys and their struggles, not the heartache that we as their loving wives face. You see, the plight of straight wives doesn't make headline news. It's not sensational, sexy, or exciting. We are more or less the "baggage" that is left behind, forced to readjust our lives by overcoming tremendous adversity. Not too many people want to hear about hardship without the glitz. And that's what we are faced with—a non-glitter pile of emotional havoc.

This prompted us to tell our stories so that we could reach the millions of women who are living this life of "emotional isolation" thinking that they are the only ones in this situation. While there are numerous support networks for gay men coming to terms with their homosexuality, there are limited avenues for women who are left behind to deal with the aftermath. But although the resources are limited, they are there if you know how to find them. All you have to do is write me at Bonkaye@aol.com and help will be on the way.

The stories you are about to read were compiled in no special order except the order they were received in. Some are stories of hope; others are stories of anguish. They are all stories of pain—the pain we feel as straight wives.

Story 1. My Story - Shelina

I can still remember the day when my seemingly ordinary life all came crashing down in a heap around me. It's funny how you can remember some of the worst moments in your life in full bright color detail. It is as if every minute is scorched on your brain. Why can't we remember the good days that way? There are plenty of really incredible days that are not much more than shadows in my mind. Just as a negative comment never seems to leave you behind, they elicit such a strong emotional response from you that you can't help but to remember them and run them over and over and over again, like a tune that you just can't get out of your head. This is one of those defining moments—one of those moments that you know that your life will never be the same again.

Miguel had been acting strangely for some time now. I tried in vain to figure out what was wrong; he insisted that he didn't know. I couldn't help but feel that he wasn't telling me the whole truth, but I didn't want to pressure him because I knew that it wouldn't do much good. He was slipping away from me and there was nothing that I could do.

We had been married for a good 10 years by this time. For the most part, things were very good. We got along great. For the first few years we had fights; shoe-throwing crazy fights (okay, so I was the one that threw the shoes!). But for the most part things were great. Part of the problem was his family. He is Hispanic and has a very large family. I am what you might call an all-American white girl and have a small family. We would often go visit his family as mine lived out of state. I never really felt very comfortable at these gatherings. There were always many people, and usually they all spoke Spanish.

My being from a small non-Spanish speaking family made it hard for me to feel part of the group. I often would often end up in some corner of the room, trying to disappear. Needless to say I was very bored at these gatherings. I never wanted to go.

Gradually we came to an understanding that he would go visit them alone most of the time and I would come when it was an important event. You know- holidays, birthdays, christenings that sort of thing.

Our little arrangement worked very well. I got to do what I wanted and he got to do what he wanted. Little did I know that this independence that I granted him would help prolong our marriage!

Months and years went by and slowly we became more and more like roommates that just happened to sleep together. Sex and intimacy seemed to leak out of our relationship until gradually we were barely having sex once a month. I had gained some weight over the years and I was certain the reason for the lack of desire on his part was because I was hideous to him. He assured me that this was not the case but that he was feeling very pressured from work and just didn't feel up to it. I wouldn't describe myself as aggressive when it comes to sex so I accepted his answers and suffered in silence.

We carried on this way for years. I suppressed my sexual desire and pretended nothing was wrong. It's amazing how well your mind can protect you. You can think up all kinds of reasons for why something is happening. You can even pretend like it isn't happening at all. Until something comes along and hits you smack in the head. Well that's not really true, you can still keep pretending at least for a little while and that's exactly what I did!

Miguel had recently started spending a great deal of time on the computer. He was using the Internet to chat online with people at all hours of the night. I would sometimes ask him whom he was chatting with. He would always tell me some guy from here or there. I thought, "He is making some online male friends. That's nice. Guess I don't have much to worry about it much because he is not chatting with woman." I remember thinking that it was kind of strange that he was chatting with men. I have chatted online myself before and unless I was chatting with my mom or sister; I have never had a female contact me to chat.

2

One afternoon, I was doing some research on Miguel's computer. I wasn't trying to snoop on him, just doing my thing. During my time on the computer, I just happened to notice some of the web sites that he had been visiting from the history that was pulled down from the address field. I felt like someone had sucker punched me in the stomach. The blood rushed from my head and I felt as if I would faint. He had been visiting gay porn sites! My mind grasped at feeble excuses as to why he would be visiting these sites. Despite my horror, I had to see what else he had been looking at. I checked all of the history from 2 or 3 weeks back. I began to feel a coldness creep over me as I saw what he had seen, what he had been searching for and what he had downloaded.

I called my best friend, hoping that she could give me some guidance as to why he might be looking at these things. She was a therapist; she would know, right?

"Well maybe he was just curious" Sara said, after I finished spilling my guts to her. "Some males go through a period in their life when they are curious as to what that is about" she explained. "Why don't you ask him? I am sure that there is a perfectly good reason why he was there."

"What the hell am I suppose to ask him?" I cried to her."' I was just wondering…Are you gay?' Oh, what am I going to do?" I sobbed to her.

"You are going to have to approach the subject very carefully. He may deny the whole thing. I am sure it's more than what you think it is." Sara replied.

"I don't think so. You didn't see what he had been looking at and what he was searching for. It was more than curiosity." I said.

Later on that evening, I tried to ask him. I really tried, but the words just wouldn't come to my lips. I started thinking about my life and our life together and I knew that if I brought it up, that would all come to end. I wasn't ready for that. Would I ever be ready? Probably not, but I didn't want to be the one that brought about the end. So I did what I do best and kept my mouth shut. I started thinking up more great excuses as to what he was doing. He has a crazy friend that thought it would be funny to put that stuff on his computer, he "accidentally" went to that site and clicked on all those links and pictures, he really was just curious and was just "looking". See? Your mind is very helpful when it comes to protecting your sanity.

Not long after I attempted to confront him about what I had seen, he came to me and asked me how he could empty the cache and history on his computer. I told myself that he was just asking because he was curious about his computer maintenance, but I really knew that he suspected that I had seen something that I shouldn't. Things were not looking up.

For months after this episode we kept up our little game. I started *trying* to be a more attentive wife…*trying* to think up things that we could do together after work and on the weekends…*trying* to be more involved with his life. We had been drifting apart for a while and this was probably what the problem was. We just weren't doing enough stuff together. I am great at trying to fix things. Maybe I just wasn't woman enough. I started exercising more and eating better, actually started losing weight. But the more I tried to fix it, the more things seemed to get worse. I was really starting to get scared.

Miguel decided that he really needed to do something to kind of get his life back in order. He was not doing well at work, he wasn't getting along with his family, and things were just getting worse and worse at home. He was spending more time away from home as well. It was as if he was trying to escape his problems.

He decided to attend a seminar that helps you to really get in touch with yourself and helps you break through any walls that may be holding you back from what you want from life. I myself had actually attended this seminar as well at an earlier time in my life. I found it to be very helpful and I enjoyed the experience but had no desire to attend again. Miguel attended it before as well, but he wanted a refresher course.

I was really against his going. Something inside me said that when he came back from this seminar, we would no longer be together. I didn't know how or why, I just knew that would be the case.

The seminar is fairly intensive. You go Friday evening, all day Saturday and all day Sunday. The location was a distance from our home so he chose to stay at a nearby hotel to make it easier to get to the class on time. I can honestly say that it was one of the longest weekends of my life. I spent most of it in a fog-like stupor. A blanket of dread settled at the bottom of my stomach. Something was going to happen all right—something bad. I don't think I have ever felt so out of control in my life. There was absolutely nothing I could do. It was as if I was in a speeding car, barreling down a winding highway and I could clearly see the cliff in the distance, advancing at an alarming rate.

He would call me each evening after he finished the day. He assured me that all is well and he was having a great time there. He was really learning a lot about himself and he was very glad that he attended. It all sounded innocent enough but my foreboding was still very strong.

At long last, he finally came home late Sunday evening. I could tell by the look on his face that all was not well. As a matter of fact, it could not be further from well. After much hemming and hawing he slowly came out with what he had to say.

"I'm um, well, see the thing is, the thing that I found out about myself, is that um, well, I guess you could say that um, well I wouldn't say gay but I am sort of, well I guess bisexual" Miguel stuttered and puttered. He actually started crying! I had only seen him cry one other time in our life and it was nothing like this.

I remember just sitting there in our bed just staring at the wall. My thoughts were all in a whirl. I just couldn't believe that this was happening to me. I mean you hear about this sort of thing happening to other woman all the time, but not me! Not my husband. How could this be? And what was I going to do? I could feel the numbness coming on and my breathing was shallow. Was I actually going to pass out?

"The thing is, I have always kind of suspected this of myself but I never could accept it. It's really been in my face in the past few months. I love and care for you too much to keep doing this to you. I really haven't been fair to you at all." Miguel was still crying. I could see the pure anguish in his face. I could see how much this was tearing him up.

"Whatever you want to do is what we will do. If you want to split up we will if you want to stay together, that's what we will do. Whatever you want."

He was looking at me, waiting for some sort of response. What could I say? I could see my world spiraling down, down, down. Everything that I had hoped for, everything that I had dreamed about smashed like nothing more than rickety old furniture. I knew that I could not stay with him, knowing this information. I knew this when I first saw what he was looking at on his computer. Isn't that really why I didn't ask him about it? I didn't want the illusion to end. I had all these little clues smack in my face and what did I do? I stuck my head in the sand. If I pretend like if it isn't there, then it isn't!

He continued on, "I just wanted to let you know that I have never cheated on you. Not with anyone. I would never do that to you. You know that don't you?

I nodded to him; yes I knew that. Despite all of this crap he was laying in my lap, despite this horrible, horrible news, he was and is a very decent man...a very good man...a very loving man. I knew he would never do something like that to me. Maybe I was being naïve here, but I don't think so. And really, would it really do me any good to think otherwise?

I felt so helpless. This isn't real. I am going to wake up tomorrow and discover that this was all a very bad dream, well maybe not dream; nightmare is a better word for it. As much as my brain wanted to shut down and go away from all this craziness I knew I had to get through it. "Just take as long as you need to think about this and decide what you want to do. I know that this is a lot to put on you and you have much to think about" he said.

Think about it? Did I really need to think about it? I mean I love Miguel, with all my heart, but could I really just go along with this little charade any longer? Every time his cell phone rang I would wonder who he was talking to. Every time he went out the door, I would wonder who he was meeting. Would there ever be a moment when I could trust that he wasn't meeting up with a man? The answer to that question is a big fat NO! Is that anyway to live? Well maybe for some people that would be ok, but I am not some people. I love myself too much to do that. I would never have any peace. So really there was only one answer to this problem.

After some time, I was finally able to attempt speech. Up until this point in my life I don't think that I had ever felt so hopeless in my life. When it came right down to it, I had only once choice. I had to leave him. If I wanted to keep my sanity and my self-respect, it was the only thing I could do.

"The thing is, I already know what I have to do. I can't stay with you. I know myself and I know that I could never be comfortable with you knowing this information. You know I love you dearly but I would go insane with worry and doubt." At this point I was crying. I was finally realizing that this was not a dream. I couldn't just wish myself out of it. It was really happening.

Miguel then said, "Do you want to divorce me?" in a very small voice.

Real fear went through my heart at those words. I hadn't even considered that. It was just too much all at once.

"Well", I said, "Let's just see what happens later on. We can always get a divorce later if it comes to that."

We started making plans a few days later. We need to get a place for me to live. We decided that I should move first and then we would sell the house and he would move later. A few months later I had a townhouse and half of the furniture. For months I would cry and cry and cry every night until I would literally fall asleep from exhaustion. It was a very low part of my life. I was lonely and scared. Yes I was utterly lonely.

Three years later, Miguel and I still keep in contact. He has been my best friend for years and I just couldn't imagine life without him in it in some small way. We just signed the divorce papers last November. I have just recently started seriously dating someone steady for the last 8 months. I am finally learning what it is like to be with a straight man after all these years. Let me tell you, I am loving it!

Story 2: Broken Promises And Shattered Dreams
by Cindy B.

I met and married the man of my dreams at nineteen years old. He pursued me relentlessly until I said "yes". He was handsome, funny, sweet and attentive. We were more than husband and wife – we were soul mates and best friends. Unlike many couples that we were friends with, we almost never fought. Our life started out in a whirlwind as he had joined the Navy and I became pregnant with our first child. So off to California we went. I had never been away from my childhood home in Iowa really before this and so everything was both exciting and scary. We lived in Mt. View up by San Francisco for 3 years and this is where my son Josh was born. We then moved to Hawaii for 3 years which during that time my second son Chad was born. After Hawaii we moved back to the California living in Chula Vista around the San Diego area. The whole military experience is one I won't forget because of many reasons but specifically it taught me how to become tougher than I had been before. I had learned to live away from home across the country while my husband was gone out of the country on 6 month deployments. These were hard to endure but I learned to get through them. I think living so far away from all family for those 9 years also brought my husband and I closer than either of imagined it would. I had the fairytale marriage, the Cinderella story, the life so many envied and wanted for themselves.

After "J" got out of the Navy we came back to Iowa to settle. He got a good job and pursued another one in the meantime. There was a company he had read about just starting out and the building was not even completed yet. But he somehow got their attention and they hired him starting out at the bottom. We moved a few times while he climbed the corporate ladder. I stayed at home and did in-home childcare to help supplement income for bills. This way I could be there with my boys as they grew up. I had done the childcare thing while we were in the Navy as well. He liked that I was at home and he took good care of all of us. He was very smart and charismatic and everyone liked him. I don't think he had a single enemy in the entire world. I think this also helped him get to the top of the company.

He then started getting sought out by bigger and more nationally known companies that wanted him to go to work for them. He took a job with one for a lot more money than he was making but it would mean he would have to travel. I wasn't thrilled with that aspect but he was so excited and it was good money. Besides I had learned about separation and being alone in the Navy hadn't I? Also, I was home now and there was family near by.

My husband was always so sweet and attentive. He never forgot holidays, birthdays or our anniversary and he always did them up big. We would almost always go out to dinner somewhere romantic. Hell, we were so in love that we even renewed our wedding vows when we celebrated our 15 years of marriage. This was no small deal either as it was in full dress. I wore a beautiful white gown with sequins and very form fitting. He wore an elegant black tuxedo and looked stunning. Our boys acted as his best men and I had my Mother there by my side. We remarried at the famous Little Brown Church that my parents had wed so many years earlier.

We had a reception and spent the night in a hotel nearby. The wedding video shows him staring at me as I walked down the isle and his eyes grew brighter the closer I got. He couldn't take his eyes off me and the video shows him smiling uncontrollably. He loved me so very much and I adored him just as much if not more. It was all so magical, so very much of what dreams are made of. I really felt like Cinderella during the ball. I didn't think life could get much better than this and I knew how lucky I truly was to have it all. I had the wonderful husband, the boys that excelled in school, we taught High School Sunday

School at church, and we had good friends and family. It was perfect!

The next five years went pretty much routinely. He would be home most of the time and then travel for a week here and there or sometimes just a weekend. As a family we became used to it, and we continued our lives. The more successful he became the more we enjoyed. We had a beautiful house in a nice neighborhood. We had a sports car, a cabin cruiser speed boat, and put in an in-ground pool in the backyard. We did all the fun things families do together like picnics and vacations as well as boating and swimming.

I remember us having lots of parties. We were the place everyone wanted to go to and hang out. We had enclosed the porch (which was huge) and made it into a bar and billiards and game room. We had lots and lots of fun. Our boys were doing great in school. Our oldest son Josh had graduated from high school lettering in academics and received a full scholarship to a local prestigious college. He achieved a 3.9 GPA all through his high school years, and I was not worried about college. He wanted to do something in politics or be a politician someday. My youngest son Chad was just finishing up his senior year in High School. Although he didn't have the grades his brother enjoyed, he still was doing very well. He had good friends, and was active in things outside of school.

We were nearing the end of December of 2003 and had decorated the house by cutting down a live Christmas tree, something we did every year – a family tradition. We would wonder around the tree farm looking for just the right one for us. Then we would take it home and decorate it with all the decorations we had acquired over the 20 years we had now been together. Our 20th wedding anniversary was right before Christmas, and as always, he didn't forget. This year he took me out for a romantic dinner and gave me a diamond tennis bracelet. Then less than a week later we celebrated Christmas. It was always so festive watching the kids open their gifts, even though they had now grown into young men.

My mother had died about four years earlier, and I missed her dearly. My father had died while we were still in the military, and I still remember the tearful flight home for the funeral. I no longer had all the family surrounding me, but I still had my immediate family to love and love me. I still had my husband and children. I was so very happy.

The past year had been much like the others before it except that he had now taken up playing Solitaire on the computer when he was home. He told me it helped relax him and reduce the stress he felt from the job. I had no reason to think otherwise so I let him play.

It was the day after Christmas and all the craziness of the holiday was now behind us, and we were on to New Year's. We always brought in the near year in the same way with a countdown to midnight and a kiss. The words "I love you" were spoken aloud, and an embrace so tight I can still feel it now. I started trying to figure out where we could go for this New Year's celebration and went to the office to run some ideas by him. I wanted to see if he had something new that we could do that we hadn't before. When I went into the office he was playing Solitaire as he often did. He was kind of quiet and didn't really want to talk about any of that right then. So, I left the room and went to the kitchen to get him something to drink as a surprise.

I came back to the room but something was not right. As I gave him the soda I noticed he was jumpy and a little edgy. He was just playing a game so what was the big deal? But I also noticed he had put the playing screen up quickly, and he had been doing something else before I came in. The cards on the game were in the exact same place as when I first came in and left. What was he doing? I thought to myself, he must be working on a surprise for New Year's for us. He wanted to do this on his own and then see my excitement of what he had planned.

He gulped down the drink and stood up to take his shower. He left up the game so he could finish it later. Once he went into the bathroom and I heard the shower turn on, curiosity got the better of me. I had to know what he had up his sleeve and what surprise he had for us. After minimizing the screen with the game on it, I saw he was composing a letter…a letter to me. I still heard the shower so I knew I was safe so I started to read.

It was at this moment my world as I knew it ended. My heart started to race and my head was swirling and hurting. I knew I couldn't read it all before he was done, so I printed it and put things back as they had been. I took the letter and locked myself in the other bathroom and sat down on the floor and read. The letter was to me alright. The letter told how sorry he was that it had taken him this long to tell me but it just never seemed to be the right time. Not the right time? To tell me what?

I read further and there it was. He said he was GAY. He said he knew it since childhood but felt that society would not accept him and would reject him. He knew he would not be able to get where he was today as a gay male. He also thought his family would disown and ridicule his lifestyle once they found out.

My heart dropped like a brick to my stomach and I felt sick. I felt the tears welling up in my eyes and then quiet sobbing. I remember just saying "no, no, no" over and over again becoming louder. Panic enveloped me as I knew life was never to be the same once the words on that paper had been read. If only I had left things be and had not gone in the office and been curious. But that would only have prolonged the inevitable. After all, the letter was to me.

I heard the shower stop and then the door open. I got up from the floor where I sat and went straight to him. I pushed the paper in his face as I cried and yelled, "What's this?" He started to cry uncontrollably. I remember his head going back and forth and his eyes shut while he bawled. He had no intention of me reading that letter now—if ever. He said he never thought he would have the guts to tell me, so he wrote it, but I was not supposed to have read it. It was too late now, I knew the awful truth.

He told me that once he started traveling, he began to experiment with the gay lifestyle. He started to frequent the gay bars out of town and made gay friends. He emailed gays he met online and had a friend he had been meeting for sometime. He had a boyfriend, call it what it is. He is not a friend, a partner, or anything else. He is a boyfriend, a lover and someone he has been having sex with while married to me!

I told him he had to tell the boys and I gave him only 24 hours to do it in. He didn't want to but after a half hour of stalling, we all sat in the family room. The very room a week earlier held laughter and happy memories. Now, the room held nothing but dread, sadness and a feeling of helplessness. It was like someone died, but no one was actually dead.

My oldest son just sat there in unbelief while the younger one screamed at his father and ran downstairs to his room. He had destroyed 20 years in less than a day. I felt like my whole life was a lie. I didn't know what was real and what was simply pretended to pull off the charade he was a master of. I had NO idea he was gay. There were never any signs that I saw. I thought I married my best friend and that I would die of old age by his side.

He didn't want things to change right away around the house. He wanted to still live there and still share a bed but without sex. I remember thinking he must be crazy and told him he had to move out as soon as possible. I couldn't sleep in the same bed anymore even though we had for 20 years been side by side. He was a stranger to me now, I didn't know him anymore. He slept on the couch for the next few days until he packed up a U-Haul and moved out.

I remember watching him from a window inside the house while he put things in the van. It was so sad; a feeling of emptiness filled me. My head was clouded and I felt like I was drugged even though I didn't so much as touch a beer from the time I learned the truth. I knew I had to keep my wits about me as much as I could. Once I had learned the truth, I noticed things I hadn't before. He liked to lie for the sake of getting away with a lie. I heard him lie over and over to people on the phone about things that really didn't matter. It was all so strange, and then I wondered how many lies he had told me.

Going to get tested for HIV/Aids is a memory I wish I could forget. I remember going in and everyone looking at me as if I was different. I remember telling the woman drawing my blood my story and watched as tears welled up in her eyes. I honestly thought she knew something I didn't, and that I was going to die. I was going to pay the ultimate price for my husband's betrayal and lies. The tests game back Negative and that was a big weight off my shoulders and heart. It was one of the longest weeks I ever had to wait.

Once he was gone, I fell into a depression. I forgot to eat as I wasn't hungry, and I slept all the time. I hated waking up to a new day. How is it that the world went on as if nothing were different? The sun continued to shine, and people went about their lives in spite of my life ending. I wanted to die. I started to research on the computer how to commit suicide with the least amount of pain and mess. I just wanted it to all end and to all be over. I didn't want to face the world all alone.

I never had a job except for doing childcare in the home. What skills did I have? How was I going to pay for the house and the utilities? I didn't know how to do a lot of the "guy" things that needed done around the house. I was scared to death. My heart was also broken into a million tiny little pieces and there was no glue or patience going to put it back together. So, each day I planned my death a little bit more until I had the method down.

But then I started to worry about if I botched it up and was left a vegetable. I didn't want that kind of burden left to my boys. I didn't want to see them have to decide whether or not to take me off life support someday. If I killed myself, it had to go right and work. There could be no mistakes.

I started to seek out sights on gay husbands/straight wives. I was surprised to find out I was NOT the only one this happened to. There were plenty of us, and I started to read more and more. I think this was what saved my life—that and my belief in God. I no longer wanted to kill myself and started to put my life back together. I found a good lawyer and obtained my divorce. I wrote up a resume and sent it out to hiring companies in the area. I knew how to type fast and had gone to college in California for a year. I put myself together each day even when I didn't feel like it. I did the hair, the makeup and put on the clothes. I had to do this in order to make it another day and to feel better.

He filed bankruptcy even though I begged him not to. He was putting all his obligations and old life behind him. I couldn't take over the expenses on my income and had to follow suit. I lost the house, the car, my husband, my family, my life, the last 20 years just like that. It is funny we started our lives out with nothing but love and food stamps and rose up to having the world shine on us and all we did. Everything he (we) touched turned to gold. Now here I was back to where I began with nothing. But honestly, money and material things meant nothing to me without my husband. I would have traded everything I had just to have back that boy I married 20 years ago. I remember how innocent and fun and ambitious he was. I knew my life was going to be one like no other, but I had no idea it would end like this.

I was offered a job at a nationally known corporation and have worked there for over 2 years now. I moved into an apartment and bought a good used older car. He moved in with the same boyfriend he had when I found out he was gay and they are still together and living 200 miles from me. I never talk to him, and he has little and next to nothing to do with our boys. I think he came and took them to lunch this past Christmas for a total of one hour.

The boys have probably suffered as much as me if not more in some ways. My oldest boy started drinking (getting 2 DUI's) and quit college. He lost his scholarship due to not attending. He then lost his job and his car. He just stopped caring about things he used to love and dream about.

My youngest son started hanging out with the wrong kids. He didn't graduate from his High School instead getting a GED. He ran off to another state for awhile and got into trouble with the law. He is still going to court to get things straightened out. He smokes cigarettes like a chimney (both boys do), but he also does drugs. It seems like both boys are so lost and can't come to terms with their father's choices and lifestyle. The youngest son told me the only time he is happy is when he is sleeping or high. It breaks my heart to see how both of them have let this situation change their lives for the worse. I just pray to God things improve and get better for both of them.

My ex's mother and sister did disown him as did most of the rest of the family. They couldn't accept his lifestyle and the deception he lived for 20 years. His mother said it best when she said "cheating is cheating, even if it was with another man" when you are still married.

I was horrified to find out he was gay but more upset that he stole 20 years of my life. Had I known how it was going to end I would never have married him even if it was a good life during those years. I wanted to be with someone I could love and be with for my entire life. I thought about how I wouldn't have my boys if I hadn't married him. But truth is, I would have had them anyway, just with a different father. This would have been a father that would have been there always for them just as my dad was for me. A man who would become a Grandfather while I enjoyed be a Grandmother someday.

Hindsight is 20/20 and was for me as well. Maybe I was just too close to the picture to see what was actually in it. I remember friends telling me they knew "J" was gay just by his actions. I saw nothing. I did find out that a lot of friends and even a neighbor were gay. I knew about the neighbor but not the friends. Now, I can look back and figure out who they were. There is one friend of "J's" that I know is gay and is married and has kids. He is living the very lie that my ex was. He is going to ruin lives someday and it is just so sad to know what awaits this wife and mother and kids.

I think one of the best things I did was make him move out. It is so hard if not impossible to heal if you continue to live the lie with the gay spouse. It is like having a sore that tries to heal and scab over but someone keeps picking at it until it bleeds. This happens over and over until what you end up with is just a big scar. This holds true with the woman that stays with a gay man. You can't let the wound heal with him living in the same house.

I know I wouldn't be as strong and as independent as I am had I let him stay with me. I learned how to do all the things he once did and sometimes I did it better. You really feel a sense of pride when you finish up a fix-it job or something he used to do for you. There is real power in being able to do for yourself. The boys are on the right track now, but it was so scary for awhile. That age is unpredictable and there is no "right" time to come out of the closet to your children. It is going to hurt at any point they find out. I have had to be both mother and father to them and had to be strong. One of the most touching moments I have ever encountered was when I overheard my oldest son talking to a friend on the phone. He was telling him how his mother was his hero and he couldn't believe all that I had been through and survived. I started to cry. It was at that moment I knew I had done the right thing.

A year after my marriage had ended I met a man that I thought was the one to help me love again. We had much in common as I skydived and he flew planes. He had a great sense of humor that was contagious and we fed off each others quick wit. But, tragedy struck again when he died in a plane crash. He was flying a new plane he had just bought and no one knows what happened but he went down. I was supposed to be in that plane, but I wasn't. I loved him and miss him but I know he is with God now.

STRAIGHT WIVES: SHATTERED LIVES

Today, I am with a guy who is both a firefighter and a mechanic. You can't get much more manly and macho than that (smiles) can you. He is very sweet and caring yet so very different than "J" was. I can see now the difference between gay and straight better. My boyfriend is always holding my hand and likes to kiss a lot and the bedroom is a playground. He and I have the best sex I have ever had in my entire life. My ex would kiss me without any tongue and oral sex was taboo and gross. The bedroom was more routine (always the same) although it was regular. I am happy again, but a little more cautious with my heart. I refuse to clam up and not live and enjoy life because of what has happened to me. I feel I have lived several lifetimes in my 44 years and the best ones are still to come.

The healing process is not an easy one, nor does it happen quickly. I am still healing and I still have times when I feel like it all happened to me yesterday. It may sound cliché', but only TIME helps make things better. Don't hurry out to find a replacement husband or boyfriend. You can't do anything good for a relationship until you can at least be at peace with your new "normal" in your new world. Everything will be different as if seeing everything through a new pair of eyes. Try to do things for yourself and try to be independent. With every challenge you overcome or problem you can fix by yourself there is a wonderful feeling of accomplishment…and life will seem a little better. And if you are religious, lean on your God and take comfort in prayer. I would say surround yourself with people, but I found my times alone a welcome alternative to always having to be busy and with others. Life does go on and you too will go on with it. It is your life and you need to make *your own* happiness and not depend on someone to do that for you. God Bless!

Story 3. "In and Out of the Closet" by Sally T

I grew up on a cotton farm in West Texas and went off to college after graduation from high school. My sophomore year I met Brad and we were never apart. We got married two years later. We had two beautiful daughters and my life was what I had always dreamed. I dropped out of college to get married and raise my family.

After the birth of our second daughter, I began noticing that Brad was beginning to act depressed and he had become disinterested in me. I would cry at night wondering why he never wanted to make love to me anymore. His explanation was that he was taking care of our older daughter and I was nursing and needed time with the baby. He also told me that we were always fighting, and he didn't enjoy making love when we were mad at each other. This excuse lingered for years.

I went through years of not knowing what was wrong with our marriage and I guess I just went through the motions. Brad always seemed to be depressed about his job and would get happy again for a while when he got a raise. His job seemed to be the problem at that time. His boss promised him his job when he retired, but a closure of another office caused a new person to be brought in instead. Brad became more and more unhappy.

He decided to put in for a job in the main office that was located in Austin, two hundred miles away. He applied and got the job. The girls were 9 and 12 years old. He moved into a efficiency apartment while I stayed behind to sell the house. At that time I was working full-time.

It took six months to sell the house and Brad still had not found us a house in Austin and he became more and more depressed that we could not afford a house as nice as the one we were living in. The girls and I moved into an apartment waiting for Brad to find a place in Austin. One weekend Brad came home and announced that he hated Austin and he knew we would also and that the schools were awful and we would be better off staying here. I was devastated and cried all weekend. I did not sleep at all and just cried. I told him that he would have to tell the girls and that I was not willing to do that for him. He cried and cried and wouldn't come out of the bedroom. Finally it was getting late on Sunday and I finally told him to JUST leave. And he did.

The years began ticking away. Brad came home less and less and I cried more and more. He would come home and I would beg him to move back or let us move to Austin. He would not have it. I knew that if I pushed, it would make matters worse. I knew that Brad was stubborn and would not give in. I think I cried for about four years until I finally decided that I needed to live with it or get a divorce. Brad continuously said that he loved me and didn't want a divorce. He even applied for a job here in his old office once, so I believed him.

I began to make excuses for him and support him when anyone talked negatively of him. He would always come home but we were never permitted to go see him in Austin. He had found a roommate and they moved into together to save money because it was extremely expensive to live in Austin. He had seen Joe in the apartment complex and knew him from home, where he was a schoolteacher. Joe was now divorced and living alone in Austin. Joe had been married, divorced and had a son. Again I never questioned this.

Through the years of living apart, I became very independent and finally became so numb to my feelings towards him that I was happy and really did not want Brad coming home. I was pretty well isolated from everyone. I enjoyed being alone and when Brad did come home, I felt like we had to do what he wanted to do. I had hoped and prayed that one day I wouldn't care if he came home or not. Many times he would call on Thursday night and tell me he felt bad or the weather was going to be bad and he was not coming home that weekend. I would be devastated since I had looked forward to him coming home for weeks.

Even though I was busy with the kids and I was around people daily, I felt so alone. I wanted companionship so badly and when Brad did come home, he was busy in the yard, busy fixing things and never eager to be with me. When I look back Brad never came home unless the girls were going to be there. Never did he come home to see me. There was one time when he decided to come home and both girls were not going to be here. I was so excited, but again he managed to find an excuse and not come. I felt like another daughter when he was around. I got the same type of attention and affection. I never got the love and attention I longed for. I was made to feel like my sexual appetite was abnormal and extreme.

Several years later, I got a terrible shock. Quite by accident, I found out that Brad's roommate, Joe was gay. A co-worker mentioned his name and said that he was gay, and he had moved to Austin where people would be more liberal and understanding.

I called Brad and told him what I had found out and that he should move out immediately and we would find a way to make the money stretch and he should get his own place. I told him that we would be able to travel to see him and he wouldn't have to do all of the traveling. He was amazingly agreeable. I told him that I knew that he and his mother worried about appearances and I knew that he would never live with a gay man knowingly. And that people would think he was gay too. Several days later, Brad told me that Joe was sorry that I found out that way, and Brad never brought up moving again.

I could write and write about all of the things he said and did and was not here for. He was giving us money and he believed that was his job. He became angry if I even suggested that the girls might be scarred for life from our situation. He was doing his part. Little did I know that through the years, my daughters had worried that their dad might be gay. They felt abandoned as I did. After all, he was never there for them during important events much less minor events.

I lived with the knowledge that he was gay for a long time. I needed the financial security I guess, but I still had it in my head that I wanted to keep my family together. I did not want to face the truth. There were red flags all around me. I had stayed married, lived separately and tried to keep the family together for over 15 years.

I became more and more unhappy with being married and knowing that Brad would never be truthful. He decided in 2001 to retire and of course the original plan was for him to move back home when that happened. As usual, that didn't happen. We were not invited to his retirement party and that really burned me inside. He told me about a great job he could have in Austin that would pay big money and he could pay off our daughter's college loans. This was the last straw. If I ever had a doubt, this was the RED FLAG that I could not ignore. We began to argue more and more and Brad began to make his plans to work his new job. We didn't speak for over a year during this time and wrote very hurtful emails to each other. He felt that I was to blame for any unhappiness the girls went through, I was being selfish, I never treated his mother fairly and he never liked my family. With all of this and the support of my two daughters, I finally had the courage to tell him that I wanted a divorce. At first the divorce started out very ugly, but we finally agreed on everything after I threatened to tell the girls what he had said to me one night over the telephone. Brad wanted to sell the house and not let me keep it because he was sure that I was moving in another man into HIS house. The divorce became final the day before my 54th birthday.

Our oldest daughter eloped that year and we had a big party for her and her new husband here. Brad came and that was the first time that I had seen him in over a year. We began talking and getting back to being around each other again. I even allowed Brad to come to my house and visit the girls when they were here visiting. My family adored him and he was here during my family reunions.

The first year after the divorce, Brad had a massive heart attack and the girls and I went to see him. It was then that we decided together that Brad was definitely gay. We saw his friends coming up to see him at the hospital. After that trip, I found a book written about gay/straight marriages and a support group to talk to. This information was what I desperately needed and wanted for years but never found. I thought I had accepted the truth, but this threw me into a complete tailspin.

Today, Brad is a very lucky man because his daughters still want a relationship with him. I have corresponded with Brad and told him that I have known the truth for a long time and his daughters deserve an explanation. He finally admitted that he is gay (in his own way). I am one of the few women to ever receive the truth and have this kind of closure. But this knowledge again threw me into turmoil. I must still be in denial after all of these years.

I found some old letters I wrote to Brad, but never mailed. I think this one probably tells of the anger and hurt I went through. At times I seem to become overwhelmed by frustration and anxiety over our relationship. I think back of all of the years you have refused to talk to me and seem to be hiding things from me. I wonder why I have stuck around and not gotten away to find happiness elsewhere. When I asked you a question (being gay), I never got an answer only a question back - that I was made to feel guilty for even asking.

You have a talent to turn things around on me, making me feel like I am the one who is unreasonable. But I don't believe it anymore. Years ago, it was always me that wanted to make love, and you made excuses that you weren't in the mood because we were always mad and fighting with each other. But now I see that it wasn't me at all.

I have spent all of the years wondering if we could ever save our relationship. I get angry thinking that you refuse to tell me the truth and let me get on with my life. I deserve more than this. Years of making excuses for you never being here, and of you asking me if I think you should come for events in our daughter's lives. I won't beg anymore.

I deserve the truth, even if the truth is only why you covered up living with a roommate that is gay. Why did you feel it necessary? I want the truth, and if you refuse, then you are living with the reality that the people who love you the most are the ones that you have continuously hurt. You have hurt me more than you'll ever hurt, because I have lived with the feeling of never being good enough. I feel totally rejected.

I was married for over 30 years, but I had not lived with Brad for 15 of them. I feel very sad that I did not get out of the marriage many years ago. My daughters and I are doing all right, but the scars will always be there. I have been talking and writing about my experiences. Together my daughters and I came out of the closet that he so secretly put us in with him.

Story 4. An Amazing UNEXPECTED Journey by Carol

My journey started with I was 12 years old. That is when I met my ex-husband. We were both "transplants" from different schools from out of the district, so all the "transplants" were put into one homeroom. We connected as soon as we met and became instant friends. After all, we didn't know another soul in the school, so, might as well make new friends! We soon became best friends.

Time went buy quickly, and before we knew it, we were in high school. We dated on and off through high school (mostly on) and, I must say, we had a great time in high school. All the usual teenage functions and events were so much fun. We went to the football games, dances and the proms and really had a great time.

We became engaged in our senior year. I really was not planning on getting married so soon, and, as you will learn many times in this story, I had a very hard time saying NO to any of his ideas.

Graduation came and soon we began to make wedding plans. I thought we should wait, as I wanted to go to college to become a teacher, but he convinced me that no, we should just get married and I should work for the local bank. So, of course, I did. Do you see a pattern coming?

We were married a little over one year after graduation. He would have liked it to be immediately after graduation; however the state we live in required you to be 19. The wedding was just wonderful, just like Cinderella and Prince Charming. Two hundred people in attendance, everything was PERFECT!

Then...it all changed...

Our wedding night was a disaster. I was in my little skimpy bridal nightgown, ready for a Wonderful Cinderella night! Nope—nothing. I thought, well, that's odd, it was never like this before; he was always all over me. Maybe that should have been a CLUE? However, the rest of the honeymoon was great!

Life went on, I worked in the bank, he on the other hand had many, many jobs that never seemed to last very long.

After 18 months of marriage, he decided that we should have a baby! I really hadn't thought much about having children but, again, it was his decision that I eventually agreed with. Within weeks, I was pregnant. I must admit that I was very happy with the thought of having a baby in my life. Our daughter was born and again, everything seemed great! She, of course, was the most Perfect Child in the world and he seemed like the perfect dad.

Two years went by and we had our second child. It was totally unexpected, but still a joy. Now we had the perfect family, two children, our own home and he finally had a good job! I was lucky enough to be able to stay home and raise our children. His job (or so I thought) required him to work nights, weekends and business trips.

In time, he decided that he had no outside activities so he decided to join A local theater group (funny, I don't ever remember him saying that he liked to act!) Hmm, thinking back now, he was really, really good at acting in real life, but not on the stage, because he really sucked at that!

While spending many, many, way too many hours with the acting group, he met a "new friend". He said many times that one problem in his life was he had no male friends! So, I was happy that he found a new FRIEND.

This person also was married and I had no reason to suspect anything out of the ordinary. We became fast friends with this guy and his wife. We all had children and they were all about the same age and we all got along great. We would go on day trips together and weekend vacations. We all had a great time together.

More time passed and we can now fast forward to being married for ten years. Things now were not going so well. Many times we were at each others throats. He didn't like the way I was raising the children although he just about had no interest in anything they were doing, getting him to even go to a soccer game was a chore; he didn't like the way I kept the house—no matter what I did, it wasn't good enough.

I couldn't iron his clothes the right way, if I moved the furniture around, he would change it back after I went to bed. The lawn wasn't mowed soon enough and when it was, it wasn't done correct, I could not have possibly vacuumed that day, as there were no vacuum marks in the carpet, etc. etc. etc. I couldn't do ANYTHING right anymore! I couldn't even pick out my own clothes (you're not really going to wear that are you?) If we were going out for the evening, he would even have my jewelry picked out, polished and laid out on a napkin for me to wear!! I was beginning to feel like an absolute idiot!! This nonsense went on for another 10 years.

When we were married 20 years, we were having major financial problems most of all because as I mentioned earlier, I could not say "No" to him. Whatever he wanted, he got. He dressed in the best clothes, went back to school with us paying the whole freight, ate lunches out EVERY day, went for drinks with friends after work and on and on and on. He began to think that the ATM card had a never ending supply of money. However, I still tried and tried to make ends meet while pulling money out of wherever I could while he was out wining and dining whoever. It was, as he said, "business", so, I robbed Peter to pay Paul and we ended up sunk! I'm talking dead ass broke!! There was a foreclosure on the house and creditors calling ALL THE TIME to where I wouldn't even answer the phone anymore.

At this point, he decided he should move out! Oh, did I mention that we hardly EVER had SEX. And I'm not talking just in the end. This started about 10 years into the marriage. It just became less and less and less as the years went on. I, being so naïve thought, hmm, I've only been with one person in my whole life, this just must be what happens when you're married this long… DUH!

So, in our 20th year of marriage, he moved out. I was totally, and I mean totally devastated. I never, ever, ever thought that we would not be together. He told me that if I didn't go to a counselor to find out "what my problem was" as far as finances went, that he wouldn't even THINK of coming back. So here we go again about the I can't say "No thing, I went to a counselor and guess what? After talking and talking and more talking, she said, "Do you think he's gay?" I replied, "Well, I really hadn't thought about it, but maybe". She said, "Come right out and ask him", that's your assignment this week." So, I did. Well, I guess by now you know the outcome. "No," he said, "I'm not gay, I'm bisexual" (that means GAY)...AND the "friend" from the theater group had been his "boyfriend" all along...yup, all those years! Didn't I feel like a jerk? His "friend" and his family would come over for every holiday and my ex even was even the Godfather to their new baby!

We divorced during the year or our 25th anniversary. Even knowing what I knew, I was still devastated getting divorced. I was totally heartbroken. Even the lawyer said she had never seen any client so sad to be getting a divorce.

So, the divorce went through and to end the day on an even worse note, as I left the courthouse, I had a parking ticket on my car. The perfect end to the perfect day!!

After Divorce Day, I had many, many people so graciously tell me, "We couldn't believe that you didn't know what was going on ...we did. We just didn't want to hurt your feelings!" Wasn't that nice of them? I also had many of his co-workers tell me that "we didn't want to tell you what was going on because we couldn't figure out if you knew or if you were just really accepting."

So many people want to share so many stories with you when it's way, way too late. So, in the end, unfortunately, I found out that all those late night meetings, overnight shifts and business trips were all a BIG FAT story that I fell for, hook, line and sinker. I even found out that one of his "business trips" had been to Bermuda with his "actor friend." There had been many, many more "friends" over the years.

No matter what he wanted to do or where he wanted to go, I would always agree with, for I always felt that he needed an outlet outside the home...

Well, this is my saying: I gave him enough rope and he Hung ME!!

So, now to the AMAZING part of MY JOURNEY...I HAVE survived. I have two most beautiful, grown up, married daughters who make me very proud EVERY DAY OF MY LIFE! They are raising their own children now and I love spending every single minute that I can with my grandchildren! I have a wonderful life! I own my own home, I drive a brand new car, I have traveled to places I had only read about in magazines, I have a GREAT job that I love, I have friends who love me and most of all, I LOVE ME!! I like spending time with ME! So, believe it or not, there is Life AFTER a Gay Husband.

Story 5 – Dreaming a New Dream - Kathryn's story

In my own story I grew up within a family, which had its own share of dysfunction. I had an emotionally and mentally abusive father and a passive mother whose attempts to bridge the distance between my father and his children were largely unsuccessful. In hindsight, I think my father was his own worst enemy and he didn't know how to work through the depression/anxiety that permeated our home. My mother was helpless to change anything but loved us in the way she knew how. The exposure to the emotional/mental/verbal abuse took its toll on me. I have struggled with this beginning and vowed to not let it be my legacy with my own children.

I waited to marry until age 30 and up until the moment I met my husband, I had decided that I would probably NOT marry. I wasn't going to settle for any man, and that it made sense to be single. I am not one to do things because others/society think we must. Then, I met my husband some 24 years ago now. (1982) He had a PhD, good Christian values, a secure and stable work record, he owned his own home, but most importantly, he embodied what I thought at the time was a good sense of family life, a spiritual life and he wasn't explosive/abusive/ like my dad. So in a way, he had what I thought was a healthy profile. Yes, I was physically attracted to him as he was very handsome. It was the first thing I noticed about him, his smile, his eyes and seemingly his kindness.

When we began to date it was exclusive. I was 28 and he was 29. He had no sexual history, and I had been sexually active for years. So, I was his first and only lover. He said he dated women, but in truth, there were only two others, and I met one of them. She had no interest in settling down and these many years later she has never married. She was a safe woman to date as she asked for nothing. After my husband and I dated for 14months, we eloped. We had to as he told me his mother would commit suicide if he married me because I was raised as a Catholic and he was a rigid Protestant who believed in the literal word of the Bible.

The announcement came out in a therapy session and yes, we were in therapy BEFORE marriage at my urging. We had pronounced differences sexually, spiritually and I thought we should talk about those before we married. I thought by bringing these out in the open we could move past them; that his sexual insecurity would pass with time if he realized I loved him and that I had chosen him over all others.

But, I ignored very important red flags in order to date/marry this man. He immediately made me uncomfortable about having friends outside of our relationship. ALL friends and outside interests were dropped because he was too insecure to withstand my interaction with others, and in particular, male friends. My thought: "He will be more secure after I have made a commitment to him; he will see that I "chose" him over others and then, he will feel secure." I also had to convince him to have sex with me because we were in love. He said he wouldn't have sex until we were married. He was the ONLY man I ever had to convince to have sex with me. Another flag…religious reasons or not, this man was 30. His rigidity spilled into all aspects of our lives.

We married in 1983. I was 30 and he 31. We had an okay sex life. I felt he was gaining confidence and security, trust and acceptance in this aspect of our lives. But, after we married, he and his mother would pick out clothes for me and comment on the hairstyle I would wear. My husband would correct my grammar in front of others. He would passively make it known if I didn't "look a certain way" before we went out in public. His mother, as it turns out, has a Narcissistic Personality Disorder. Much later, I learned my husband is also this way.

As mentioned earlier, my husband and I had been in and out therapy BEFORE we were married. When I was pregnant with our first son, at around 5 months into the pregnancy, he emotionally "left" the relation. I was very hurt by this as I was an infertility patient and had endured a lot to become pregnant. Finally our son was born in 1989.

My husband was jealous and hateful towards him, screaming at him and me. I became fearful he was going to abuse the boy. I got us into therapy again. It helped for awhile, and he controlled the verbal abuse towards me with the help of therapy. But, things were never the same. I felt that I had to be on guard from then on. I felt my husband pull away and "punish" me for loving my son. I couldn't understand how a grown man could feel this way toward his own son. But, it never went away. For me, having my husband and son was all I had wanted. But he took this when he emotionally abandoned me.

I became pregnant again and had our second son in 1991. He was a loving child, quiet, beautiful and all anyone could hope for. Again, my display of love and affection for this child was a sign to my husband that I couldn't possibly love my boys and him too. He further pulled away from me. Our relationship became even more strained, but I didn't think I could leave with two small children. My husband appeared depressed and anxious. Nothing could make him happy.

Over the course of our 22 year marriage, we have been with 8 therapists and the real issues were never resolved. My husband was also instrumental in having me the identifiable patient and yet, he never divulged that he was interested in men. He traveled a good deal and did very little for the day to day care of our children. His participation in therapy was to show the therapists that I was incompetent as a person and as a mother. Therapy was for me. He was the perfect husband, father and man. I just needed fixing and be made over into an acceptable wife. It was almost like being a Stepford wife in hindsight.

Why did I stay? I believed in family, my marriage vows, and for the love and sake of my two boys whom my husband resented my attention towards. In mid-life, I also began a second career as a painter when my boys were 3 and 5. I continued to work outside the home, raise the boys and begin the daunting task to become a painter at age 41. My husband resented my new interest. He said that I would never contribute anything to the field of painting- probably one of the worst things he has said to me since knowing him. Any real happiness in my life, my boys, my new career became a source of displeasure and more insecurity on the part of my husband.

Today, I am in therapy for me; working on issues which were there before my marriage and how things played out in the marriage. It's difficult to think of myself as being outside of his watchful eye; to think I am not determined by his criticism and authoritative stance. I am looking at myself as an individual, not as someone who isn't as perfect as he thought I should be. New territory for sure, but how much healthier!

It's also a good feeling not to spend my energy reassuring him and making him feel secure. That was a flag that I didn't pay attention to. I thought if I loved him enough; made a commitment through marriage, he would relax and feel confident and secure in my love. It never materialized. The children worsened his insecurities and when I turned to my new career, it was the nail in the coffin. He felt I had abandoned him and that I had done some vile thing. I don't think he ever felt secure with me as a man and given his sexual identity issues, is it any wonder?

For the last decade of the marriage, he became less and less interested in sex. He would be impotent completely by the time it was all over. He became involved in auto-erotic sex via a gay porn wrestling web site where he had posted a profile to be involved with men. I intercepted an email to a man he was going to meet when we were preparing yet another round of joint marital therapy. After that, I told him it's over and filed for divorced.

As he falls under the heading of Narcissist Personality Disorder, his tendencies to be addicted to attention and to watch himself grow older have worsened. This is a man who can't pass by a mirror without looking at himself. This recognizable personality illness is deeply resistant to therapy. All those years of therapy were for me to get better, become more, do something...and not for him.

What this man took from me is this: my sense of creating a new family (outside my family of origin) with a loving husband and children, something I had wanted my entire life; he badly crippled and hurt my own sexual identity by not being able to respond/love me in a sexual way. He eroded my sense of identity/ self and because of my own family of origin issues, I became invisible in the marriage. I assume my responsibility in the marriage for letting this happen. But the marriage was entered into under false pretenses by my husband. After all was out in the open, this man begged me to remain as his wife saying he wouldn't involve himself in the gay porn again (it happened twice) and that he would do anything if I stayed. To me the marriage was a lie and he had misrepresented himself to preserve his ego and false image of who he was/is.

Since filing for the divorce, I have never known such peace and even though financially it will be a struggle for me, I have never looked back on the decision to leave. My husband has told the boys that I haven't given him enough time to change and that marriage is forever; and that if I, Mom, would give him a chance we could remain as a family. He has enlisted his parents to present me to my boys as someone who has given up on marriage and the commitment to family. For now, I have to take that and suffer privately until such time the boys can know the truth about their father. But, I will gladly suffer a bit more for their sake, so that when the time is right, I will be fully exonerated in my boys' eyes.

Kathryn M.

Story 6. How Did This Happen To Me? By Audrey B

My story is probably very similar to many others. I joined the Navy in 1975 at the age of 17, I had a rip roaring time and dated many men over the years which I find in a way quite ironic as how did I end up with a gay one.

I met R at the age of 25 and married him the following year, the majority of our courtship was carried out at the weekends as he was away during the week. To this day I am not sure I loved him when I married him, as I had recently split up with a man I was madly in love with, but who was totally unreliable. R on the other hand was lovely, kind, and did what he said he was going to do, but to be truthful I think I married him on the rebound. I did fall in love with R and the first ten years of our marriage was good. My friends were envious of how good he was around the house and would comment on how lucky I was to have him.

The problems started soon after we got married, he was very undemonstrative. He never said he loved me or held hands or cuddled or any thing that I now realize is part of a normal relationship. At the time I did not find it particularly odd as my Father, who came from a broken home, was never demonstrative towards us or my Mother, and my mother was not the most affectionate person in the world. So after a while of trying to get R to show me affection, I just gave up. With neither party trying anymore it just got worse and worse over the years. In fact, for me sex became affection as that was the only time we ever really touched each other.

I can even remember my daughter, who was approximately 8 years old at the time saying to me that it was not like Mummy and Daddy were married as we never kissed or held hands. I even said to R. that it was like living with my brother as there was no passion in the marriage at all. It was just nice, safe and BORING! Once I joked to him that he could quite easily have an affair and I would never find out as he was working from home and he had a lot of evening appointments. Again, this was quite feasible as he was working as a financial advisor and it was normal to see people in the evening in their own homes.

As it was a drip, drip, drip over the years, we were married for almost 20 years, and nothing changed overnight I never really noticed what was happening I just got more and more unhappy and slowly my confidence disappeared. Somewhere along the line I turned from a funny, lively woman into what I called "The Grey Lady." I used to look into the mirror and see this dowdy, drab, unhappy person looking back at me. Even my blue eyes had turned grey.

R, meanwhile, I have since found out, was fighting with his own demons. He said after having feelings over the years that simply did not go away when he reached 40, and they were still there and getting stronger. He decided that he had to act on them. He started to go out and met men which led to him feeling disgusted, and he used to sit in his car and cry for hours. He then started to distance himself from us. He had it in his head that when it all came out, as it would surely do one day, then he would lose it all—his wife, his kids, his friends and his house. He started to stay away from the house more and more. On weekends he used to be out almost all day Saturday shopping, visits to the DIY store, to the service station to wash the car, anything to avoid being in the house.

I, of course, had no idea what was going on. I remember wondering why I was so unhappy. I had a lovely home, two wonderful children, and a husband that was a nice decent man whom I trusted implicitly. What did I have to be unhappy about? And not once during this period did I cry, as I did not know what I would be crying for.

The only clue I found once was an internet file that was headed "cottaging." The file was empty and I just thought that either my son or daughter had downloaded it by accident and deleted it. It never entered my head it had anything to do with R as he never went near the computer when I was in the house, and it never occurred to me that he was gay.

The night I found out, I had been to the cinema to see the first 'Bridget Jones' movie and had had a lovely evening with my sister and a friend. I got home, feeling, for me, quite happy. I got in the house and there was R, tearful and exceedingly drunk. He had drunk most of a bottle of whisky. He said he had something to tell me, and after quite a few questions I guessed, possibly as it was the only thing I hadn't asked him. He could not bring himself to tell me.

To say I was stunned, amazed, and disbelieving is a complete understatement. I had absolutely no idea. To cut a very long story short, we decided after much discussion, tears, and distress that we were going to split up. But when it came to it, he couldn't go. He said that it was only sex and that what we had and the kids and everything, it was just too much to throw away and that he would stay. Well, that worked for a while, and for a short time he became the husband I always dreamt of, attentive, touchy-feely, and demonstrative. But it did not last, and of course it all started falling apart again. After my initial feelings of elation that we were going to make it as what we had was so special and our relationship was strong enough to survive, I very quickly started going down hill. I was just so unhappy and there was this permanent feeling of dread that to this day hasn't completely gone away.

Two years after he came out to me, we split up. I had just had enough, and I wanted more out of life. I wanted to be happy again and to live—not just exist. I wanted the chance to find a man who could love me properly. We actually decided to split up on New Years Day 2004.

Our children who are 16 and 18 years old now, know their dad is gay. They did not know the real reason why we split up until my 16-year-old daughter found out by accident. She went out for the day with her dad, and she was playing with his mobile phone. She found a txt message that gave the game away. It was nothing too awful but she put two and two together and came up with the right answer. I am sad that she found out the way she did, but I am glad that they know. I had to tell my son as R could not do it. It makes my life so much easier that they both know and I do not have to worry about them finding out as it has already happened.

They are now very accepting of their Dad, although it was not always that way. My son has always been okay with it after the initial shock. The trouble he had was more with the family unit being broken apart, but he seems more settled these days. My daughter had a lot of trouble with her dad to begin with but she is fine now. They even accept their dad's partner whom he now lives with that he met after he left.

Roll on my life two years and it is so much better now. I am almost the person I used to be, although I am not sure that I will ever get back to being that person. In lots of ways I think I am much nicer now as I am nowhere near as judgmental as I used to be. I am far more tolerant and accepting of people. I read a letter in (Bonnie Kaye's) Aprils newsletter where the lady described herself as being fragile and I think that is a good description as I am too. Maybe we all are after something like this happens. I function quite well most of the time, and I am moving on in leaps and bounds. But the smallest thing can knock me off track and I get very scared of the most peculiar things, not things but experiences.

I have met a lovely man, whom I have been seeing for a year. He is attentive, affectionate, kind and making love with him is fantastic, because it is real. But this last year has been really hard as I have had to stop myself running away from him so many times, only because I have not been able to deal with my emotions. I have spent a good part of the last year waiting for him to dump me as I could not imagine why he would want to be with me. He has never given me any reason to doubt him; it is just in my head. I think I am finally beginning to settle down. I have even had the confidence to start arguing back on the odd occasion, but there is still a frightened and scared little person hiding inside.

R and I get on reasonably well under the circumstances, and I am sure that is why the children are dealing with it all so well.

However, I have one major thing that nags away at me. It is not the infidelity, or that he was putting me in danger by having unprotected sex with me because he always had protected sex with men. What I will never be able to forgive him for is that he saw the state that I was in. At one point, I ended up on anti-depressants, in the cardiac ward and basically was a complete mess—and this is what prompted him to tell me. BUT it took him so long and during this period he let me believe for all that time that it was me that was the cause of my unhappiness when he knew all along that his homosexuality was the real reason.

Story 7: Mindy's story

We were not high school sweethearts but we were best of friends. We went to a small county school - each class had less than 200 students. We all knew each other…and in rural central Indiana; we had all known each other most of our lives. It was October of my senior year, and he had graduated the spring before. We had been best of friends since early in high school. In the mid 1970's, higher education was pursued by only a few…and many were beginning to get full time jobs, move away or get married. Stan and I found ourselves together everyday. We had been together everyday for three months before our relationship turned in a different direction. We had always loved each other dearly as friends, but we were falling in love with each other. By February, we were engaged and in July, 1976 we were married in a fairy tale wedding in our Indiana small town.

Stan didn't date anyone in high school. The idea of gay men in the middle 1970's in rural Indiana was just not heard of. We rarely even thought of it. Stan was slight - at 16 he was barely tall enough to see over the steering wheel of his car. By the time we married though, he was about 5' 8" - but he still wore just a size 28" waist pants. He loved fashion and design. He was meticulous and always took good care of himself. He hated to be called 'cute' - but as a teenager, he was. He was very cute, and he was neat and clean and appealing to me. He grew to become a very attractive man and his appearance was very, very important to him. I learned very early he required as much time in the bathroom as I did, and the ironing board was always set up for perfect creases in his pants.

We had been married for less than a year when I saw the first signs of a "fiery" temper, as his mother had previously described. I remember he threw an ashtray at me - and I remember he threw a window air conditioner out of the window. To this day, I do not remember what those episodes were about...I just remember the anger. I remember an anger I had never been witness to before. I was raised in a home where voices were rarely raised.

We were married for four years before I became pregnant. We were so excited! We both hoped for a little girl. Our dreams became reality...and we became a family. Our lives as family appeared very normal - and in retrospect, at that time...it seemed pretty normal to me too. My husband changed jobs and went to work for my family business. He became the assistant manager of one of our stores in a small community about 30 miles from our home. We bought a house, and I became pregnant again two years later. We brought our second beautiful daughter home in the fall of 1982, six years after we were married.

Within a year or so, the manager left the store and Stan was promoted to the manager position. It was soon after the manager resigned that we had found out he was gay and had left his wife and two children. This was probably 1984 and it was the first time the situation had happened to someone I knew. It was about that time, that I remember the anger in our home really beginning to escalate. I was a young, stay at home mother...working hard in our home to build a safe and happy nest for our family. That is about when I began my life walking on egg shells. Stan would come home very angry some days for no apparent reason. I remember one time he was very angry because I had not cleaned the baseboards in the house. There was one warm summer morning when I was working in my garden and my daughters were sleeping in a little later than usual. My oldest awoke and came out in the yard with and joined me in my gardening - she was still in her pajamas. She had not had breakfast yet but we were enjoying our time together. He came home and became very, very angry that she was not dressed and had not had breakfast yet. It was quite an explosive episode. He left in a rage after shouting and slamming doors.

I was trying to understand what I had done wrong. What was so wrong with me?

What could I do to make him happy? I tried to cook nice meals, I tried to keep the yard and house nice, I tried to keep the girls neat and clean. Why couldn't he ever be happy with me? What was I doing so wrong?

The Oprah Winfrey show was new and I looked forward to that hour everyday. It was an early episode of that show that I first heard the term "Emotional Abuse". She was describing a lifestyle that I was living. It was the first time that I began to think this behavior wasn't really right and maybe it wasn't my fault. Logically of course, I could have those thoughts when I was alone and it was peaceful. In the middle of the rage and in the aftermath, I would sob and sob trying to understand why I had made him so mad.

We had become involved in our community and very involved in our church. The girls were growing up and it was time for a bigger house. Stan needed constant change to be happy - and a new house seemed exciting to me also. Happiness also was appealing - if he could be happy in a new house, maybe we could be okay. So we began a process that took over a year to complete. It was clear though, that the lifestyle we wanted wasn't going to be comfortable on one income. Although he really wanted me at home with the girls, he would blame me for financial difficulties - and the emotional abuse continued.

I had dropped out of high school my senior year when our relationship became more than friends. I had my GED but I knew I was not marketable for most jobs, and it was the middle 80's. Unemployment was very high. If I found a job, it would be horrible hours and I would probably have to pay most of my wage for childcare. I had always hoped for a higher education - so the year our youngest daughter started school, I did too. After two years of pre-requisites, and a lot of hard work, I was accepted into the very competitive occupational therapy program at IU in Indianapolis. Because of traffic, it was a two hour drive - one way - five days a week for two years.

Stan was very good with our girls, and he was supportive of my education. He was able to relocate to our family store in our hometown because it was closer to the girls while I was in school. He resented me for the change though. He loved his position at the store that was 30 miles away from home. In retrospect, I have to wonder if this is where he was able to co-exist with his gay lifestyle.

It was during this period of time that the abuse escalated from 'emotional and verbal' to increased violence toward objects. He kicked his foot through our oldest daughter's bedroom door and several other items in our new house had to be replaced because of his anger episodes.

The year I graduated was the year the whirlwind really began to happen. It was 1993. We had now lived in the home we had built for 5 years, so of course... it was time for a change. We sold the house and moved into a beautiful 1888 Victorian home. It was a wonderful home for two young pre-teen daughters. We worked very hard renovating the home that was highly recognized in our community. It was also the same year I graduated from OT school. I had incorporated my own independent contracting therapy business, and I was making a lot of money. I was making more money than Stan was making. During this time, one of his closest friends was hit by a car and killed. He had to be at the hospital when the body was identified. It was a very difficult time.

On a spring day in May of 1994, Stan was going to a local marina that was about 30 minutes from our home to get our boat out of storage for the summer. The route to the marina passed through a state park reservoir area. He came home from work that day without the boat. He had a terrified look in his eye. Our middle school girls were at home so he told me to please come up to the bedroom he had to talk to me.

I will never forget that day. He told me he had been arrested at the reservoir for public indecency because he had stopped to urinate. He had stopped to urinate in a cup in the back seat of his van. I believed him. I laughed it off and didn't seem to think it was such a serious problem. He seemed far more concerned than I was. He had been taken to jail, and had to have one of the guys from our local business come to post his bail.

Friday morning, the next day, when our local paper arrived, I realized this was a more serious situation than I had first thought. The headline discussed a local minister that had been arrested at the state park along with 35 other local men for public indecency because of homosexual behavior. Stan's name was not in that article that day, but it made me realize how this serious this situation was going to look. I was scared, but I believed him. I stood by him. I had no reason to doubt him.

Saturday morning the headline read "Local man among 60 arrested at state park". His name was listed in this article and many more articles that followed. The headline always started the same way…"Local Man…".

After more than six months, many newspaper articles, many dollars in attorney fees, emotional roller coasters, there were deeper relationships with the friends that stood by us while relationships ended with friends that didn't. Sitting in that courtroom that day, I was 100% sure he was "Not Guilty." I had no doubts. The story seemed odd that he was urinating in a cup in the back seat of the van. He had told me some details of the event that he didn't disclose to many people. He said a man got in the car with him and touched his arm and "came on to him."

The man was the arresting officer and said he had witnessed Stan exposing himself. It all seemed very, very odd - but I truly believed in his innocence. There were so many arrests and so much time had passed that the arresting officer couldn't clearly identify him and identified Stan as being in a van that was a completely different color than the one he drove. The attorney was very good - good enough to convince the judge…and also good enough to convince his wife. He was found "Not Guilty".

All of these transitions - the new house, my new income, his job change from the smaller community to our hometown, his friend's death, and the arrest changed him. He became so angry after the arrest. His anger became completely out of control. He began directing some of the abuse to our oldest daughter and to our pets.

I remember episodes when he pulled our teenage daughter down the stairs by her hair. i remember episodes that included kicking the dog or pushing it with his foot or a broom down the basement stairs. He continued to be very destructive with objects in our home.

Throughout our marriage - my weight had fluctuated as much as 100 pounds. I would lose the weight, and I would gain it back. In 1997, I began dieting again and quickly dropped over 100 pounds. I had wanted so much to make him happy. He seemed happy with me when I was overweight, but he made comments and statements that would hurt. I remember that he was so angry with me because I wanted to lose weight for my 20th class reunion, but I was overweight and embarrassing for his class reunion the previous year. It was a side of him I had never seen. It wasn't a short episode. it involved a lot of painful words and slamming and throwing of household items.

This kind of behavior became the norm. He would call me names and accuse me of things that absolutely were not true. He was so hateful and the words he used caused so much pain. I became so afraid. I didn't know what was going to set him off or how bad it was going to be. He would leave in his fits of rage and be gone for hours at a time. Years later I had several people tell me that during that time, he was seen at gay establishments out of town.

Stan had bought an old vintage car and was happy to have me home alone while he spent hours and hours after work with his dad on his old car. I decided to start exercising during the time he was working on his car. I became very, very committed to the exercise program and found myself working out two times a day. I would lift weights in the morning and go back in the evenings for cardio training.

I became good at what I was doing - and other people noticed me. I had become so withdrawn from family and friends, but it felt good to throw myself so completely into my body and see positive results. The abuse continued though, and it became difficult to hide. I would come to the gym with a tear stained face and there were days that the concentration needed for weight lifting was very difficult to muster.

An old flame of mine was a member of the gym. Bart was someone I dated as a teenager, just before Stan and I began dating. I was smitten with Bart as a teen and he was also attracted to me. However, I was 16 and he was 19 when we had dated, and I think the age difference had a great deal to do with us not continuing a relationship beyond dating for 6-8 months. Our attraction to each other had not changed in 25 years.

Bart and I were always drawn to each other as teens, and it wasn't any different now. We had what we described as "kismet'. He sensed my pain and noticed my tear stained cheeks. He became my friend again. I looked forward to seeing him at the gym because he made me laugh. He was positive with me and he made me feel like a woman. I felt safe and protected when I was around him. After several months of friendship our relationship changed. We became deeply involved emotionally. We fell in love with each other.

During this time, Stan became completely obsessed with my relationship with Bart. He accused me of being involved in an affair with him. At that time, our relationship had not crossed any sexual lines, so I justified that we were not having an affair. The truth is we had fallen in love and the emotional ties were far stronger than any sexual affair.

I was put through months of hell. The abuse really escalated at this point because of Stan's frustration of losing control. Stan would make horrible accusations and say terrible things that no one deserves to hear. He would storm out of the house and be gone for hours and hours. He would follow me and he would follow Bart everywhere. He wasn't spending any time at work and he became disassociated from family and friends. The police were called to our house several times because of the abuse that occurred.

One evening - in April, 1999, Stan became completely enraged. He took all of my jewelry from me because "a whore like me didn't deserve jewelry like that." He threw clothes out the window, he destroyed items in the house, and then he left. The episode involved the police. I had been involved in domestic violence groups and Stan and I had spent thousands of dollars on counseling. After that night, I became scared. I began to think I was truly in danger.

He didn't come home that night. He then moved into a hotel, and it was during that time that my affair crossed all of the lines. Stan was out of the house for about two weeks, and as a typical woman in an abusive relationship, I let him move back in. He promised it would be different.

It wasn't. The abuse continued to escalate and then in July of 1999, I confessed what he already knew was true. I was having an affair. It was definitely the worst decision of my life, not only because having an affair is morally wrong, but also because it let Stan 'off the hook'. He now believed that everything wrong with us was because of my infidelity. I agreed to continue counseling, and I stopped the affair. I quit going to the gym, and all relationships with friends in common were ceased. I didn't leave the house without Stan's permission or without him. He had complete knowledge of my constant whereabouts. I truly gave it 200%. I made a decision that if this marriage was going to fail, it wasn't because I didn't try.

Stan could not get past my affair. He became so obsessed. He continued to follow me everywhere, and he continued to follow Bart. He was constantly leaving the house for hours at a time late at night. I had no idea where he was going. The abuse continued to spiral out of control. It was becoming more and more physical.

Stan was certain I was still involved with Bart, but I honestly was not. I was beginning to understand that I had to be the one to change what was happening in my life - because as much as I wanted to believe he was going to change, it was not going to happen.

At a convention in Indianapolis, a very violent episode occurred late in the evening in a hotel room that involved the Indianapolis police. It was a horrible scary evening that left me with bruises on my neck. The police were adamant that I file charges. I just wanted the abuse to stop. I didn't press charges, and Stan ended up behaving in the typical cyclical abuse pattern of living in remorse the next day, swearing he would get better. He was making promises that I knew would not be kept, but it was too close to Christmas to leave. There was always an excuse. We had a trip to Jamaica planned for February, and we had to get that over with before I could file for divorce.

The trip went very well until the last day. Stan was always obsessed with sex, but as the abuse got worse, so did the sexual obsessions. He would get so angry at me if we didn't have sex. He would accuse me of having sex with someone else. He would say horrible things and do horrible things that were degrading and humiliating and sexually abusive. The last night of the trip ended with him keeping me up all night with his emotionally abusive words because I didn't want to have sex. I just didn't understand why it was such a huge deal. The angrier he would get, the less I ever wanted to have sex with him. I couldn't make any sense out of the situation. The next morning, the cycle continued. He promised he would change, and he was so sorry. It was the same story, different day. We hardly spoke on the flight home.

We had been home from our trip for less than 10 days when another accusing, explosive episode occurred. He stormed out of the house, and I made up my mind that this time I would not let him return. He tried to come home a few days later, and for the first time in our 25 years of marriage, I said "NO"…I was done. No more…No more bruises, no more name calling, no more violence, no more desertion…we had to end this relationship. And within 30 days I filed for divorce.

Less than a month after I had filed, Stan had become very involved in a relationship. More than a month or so passed, and our daughters had still not heard a name or met this person that he spoke of frequently without his mentioning a name or a gender. A few weeks later, he came out to our daughters. He told them the truth - he was gay and involved with another man. Sixty days after I filed for divorce, it was final. My marriage was over, and my ex-husband was gay.

My ex-husband had spent most of our married life living a masquerade - always living a life behind a facade. Many people could not believe he had abused me. They knew him and he was such a charming man - how could he do that? It is now that I realize that he was constantly living a life that wasn't who he really was. He was always trying to prove something. He was trying to prove he was a loving husband - he was trying to prove he was straight married man - he was never happy with who he really was - and thus my life was shattered in the process.

Less than a year after my divorce, I began seeing and later married Bart, the man I had the affair with. He is a wonderful peaceful compassionate man, and I am now living a very happy life and I am a very happy wife. I spent 25 years of my life trying to make someone happy that couldn't be made happy by me because I am woman and he is a gay man.

In the process, I learned that in order to be totally happy, you first must be happy with yourself. In a traditional married lifestyle, Stan could not be happy with himself…and so he blamed me and became angry at the world.

My life was shattered during the marriage because of the abuse - the emotional, sexual and physical abuse at the hand of a very unhappy gay man that chose to live a life hiding behind a wife. However, my biggest regret is that I allowed my beautiful daughters to grow up in an abusive home where they came to believe that their father's abusive behavior was acceptable. After I separated from my husband, I stopped to visit my oldest married daughter at her home. It was then I knew I had to file for divorce. When I arrived at her home that day, she answered the door with bruises on her beautiful face that were left by her own abusive husband. The reality of the legacy of abuse had come full circle for me. If I did not divorce my husband, her father, then she and her sister would continue to believe that abuse was acceptable. My infant grandson would be destined to grow up to also accept the skewed normalcy of abuse. I knew the legacy had to be stopped. My daughter and I filed for divorce from our husbands the same week.

Perhaps it seems that this a story of abuse, rather than that of woman married to a gay man. That is because my story is about abuse. The issue of my ex-husbands gay sexuality was never primary for me. The primary issue is that by hiding his sexuality behind the facade of our marriage for 25 years, by using me as his mask to cover up his true self, demonstrates a prime example of emotional abuse.

Abuse stories occasionally are topic of discussion in Bonnie Kaye's support group. I have discussed the emotional, verbal, physical and sexual abuse that I endured at the hand of my ex-husband. It seems that often there are one or two women that will respond quickly to say, "At least my gay husband did not abuse me." That concept makes me really angry! I want to shout as loud as I can, "Don't you see? Using a woman as a wife to hide selfishly behind a man's gay sexuality while depriving her of a life of true happiness is an extreme form of abuse!"

This is the message I want women to hear! Abuse is abuse - Verbal, Emotional, Physical or Sexual abuse - the results are the same. Abuse passes on an ugly legacy. If a child lives abuse, he or she is destined to become abusers or to become abused. The only way to truly stop living the legacy of abuse is to end the abusive patterns that are taught to children as normal and acceptable behavior.

Life is good for me now. I really am happy with me! I am enjoying my life as a woman now, living peacefully and very happily married to a very straight man. My grown daughters have fully accepted their Dad's homosexuality. Stan is still with the same partner. I still resent that so many people had to be hurt in the process of his inability to identify who he really is, but I refuse to let his issues continue to plague my life. I do not dwell on the fact that my ex-husband is gay, and I don't try to find answers or excuses. He is gay now, he was gay then. He abused me with words, emotions, and physical violence, but mostly, he abused me because he took twenty-five years of my life to hide behind while he tried to find himself.

Much of the person I am today is because of the life I have lived during that time, but it doesn't mean my identity has to be that of a woman that used to be married to a gay man. My identity is that of a happily married woman with two beautiful grown daughters and the best little grandson in the world. I choose to live my life surrounded by people I love and people that love me. I choose to live my life enjoying the freedom of coming and going as I please - without fear. I choose to live my life doing things that make me happy while at the same time, considering others so they are not hurt in the process of my happiness. I have learned a person cannot be responsible for anyone else's happiness and becoming happy is your own responsibility. I truly believe that happiness is grown in your own garden! And they all lived happily ever after...

Story 8: Tracy and Jeff: A Love Story

It usually happens that way; you're not looking for someone, but they come along anyway. I had been dating an Israeli man, which made a friend of mine extremely unhappy. She believed that if he was Israeli, he couldn't know how to treat a woman (turns out she was right, but that's another story)! Anyway, this friend, Loretta, approached me one day and said she knew this great guy for me. "He's Jewish, he's cute and he loves theatre, music and the arts." That should have been my first clue.

Loretta drove me crazy for weeks until I finally agreed to let her give my phone number to Jeff. It took him about three weeks to call me, and when he did, it was as if we'd known each other for years. That first phone call lasted over 2 hours! We talked about everything, from families to Broadway shows to music, etc. I knew then that this was someone special.

We remained "telephone friends" for several weeks before we met, as Jeff lived in Queens and I lived in Staten Island. Then one day he called me and said, "I just did the dumbest thing. I turned down a ride to Staten Island with my brother and he's already gone." He wanted to meet me so badly that he decided to take public transportation from his apartment in Queens to Staten Island that day. I was quite impressed by the effort.

When Jeff and I met (at his brother's house) it felt as if we had known each other forever! We just clicked. That night we hung out at his brother's house, had dinner, played Trivial Pursuit, and watched a movie. When it was time for me to leave, Jeff walked me to my car and gave me a very quick kiss goodbye. I went home humming the song, "Today I Met the Boy I'm Gonna Marry." The rest, as they say, was history. Jeff started spending every weekend at his brother's house so that we could see each other. During the week, we would spend hours on the phone. It didn't take long for us to realize that we were destined to be together forever.

My first clue that there was an honesty issue came when we had been dating for about 7 months. We were sitting in a restaurant, and the song, "How Do You Keep the Music Playing?" came on. He said this song was about us. I found that very confusing because that song was about a couple about to break up. We were so in love. So, I asked what on earth he was talking about. It was then that he told me that he had lied to his entire family, all of his friends and my family about being a college grad. He had dropped out of Queens College 2 years before that, but didn't tell anyone. His parents were living in Florida by then, so they had no idea what he was really up to. They kept sending him money for tuition, but he didn't use it for that. He basically pissed it away. Anyway, he finagled tickets to his college graduation ceremony, a cap and gown, etc. His parents came to see him "graduate." When his name didn't appear in the program, he just told them it was an error. He walked down the aisle, posed for pictures in his cap and gown, and then went out to celebrate with his family. He also accepted whatever gifts he was given by his aunts and uncles.

After two years of his mother asking him where his diploma was, and Jeff telling her he was looking into it, she decided to call Queens College herself. How surprised was she when they told her her son never graduated? Of course she called Jeff at work right away. He had no choice but to confess. His brothers were told, and, by force, he told me. If he didn't tell me, they were going to.

I stuck by Jeff. I guess not realizing the magnitude of his lie. I did make him sit down with my parents and tell them the truth. I also made him promise to go back to school to make things right. He made the promise. With this lie out in the open, Jeff breathed a sigh of relief, and our relationship continued. Unbeknownst to me, there were plenty more surprises ahead!

By the time we had been dating for seven or eight months, I decided that I was ready to take our relationship to the next step: making love. When I met Jeff, I was a virgin. It had always been my intention to wait until I had met someone that I knew I'd be with forever. I knew in my heart that Jeff was that person. Anyway, the first few times we tried to make love, Jeff's body wouldn't cooperate. We chalked it up to nerves, and figured, in time, it would happen. I thought that Jeff had been with one other woman at that point (another lie). He wasn't a virgin, but he hadn't been with any *women*; something I wouldn't find out for several years. In late June of 1988, Jeff and I did, finally, consummate our relationship. We were both very happy, and that added to the incredible closeness we already felt. For me, it was a huge step into complete womanhood. Jeff knew how big a step this was for me, and he seemed to revel in our new intimacy as well.

Two months after that first time together, Jeff asked me to marry him. I was THRILLED! We had grown into each other. Our sex-life thrived. We were ready to make this a life-long commitment. Within a few short months, our wedding plans were underway: December 16, 1989. There was so much excitement in the air. Both families were as delighted as we were. I was welcomed with open arms into Jeff's family, and he into mine. As far as everyone could tell, it was a match made in heaven.

Invitations went out the usual six to eight weeks before the wedding. Everything was progressing perfectly. I was counting the days until I became Jeff's wife. Then one day, while we were relaxing watching television, the next bomb was dropped. Jeff confessed to me that when he was in high school he had had "feelings" towards other guys. He also said he never acted on those feelings, he was sure he wanted to marry me, and that he loved making love with me. After talking to a few very close friends, I allowed myself to believe that this was a normal adolescent feeling. Since he said he had never acted on any of those "feelings" I figured it was high school curiosity that was now (obviously) in the past. How naïve could one person be? Besides, our physical relationship was amazing. He COULDN'T be gay.

55

Our wedding took place as planned. It was one of the happiest days of my life. Everyone there commented on how blissful we both were. The reception was a real party! We danced into the night with our family and friends, celebrating a "perfect union." Our honeymoon was a dream: a Caribbean cruise on a beautiful ship. The weather was perfect, the food was delicious, the shore excursions were fun and, of course, there was a LOT of sex! When we arrived home, we quickly settled into our new married routine.

In October 1992, I became pregnant with our first child. The pregnancy started off perfectly, but then, in my fourth month, I found out I needed to get a (benign) tumor removed from my ovary. What a scary time that was! Luckily, I found a wonderful doctor at Mt. Sinai Medical Center in Manhattan. He was a high-risk specialist with a great deal of surgical experience. The surgery was a success, and the rest of the pregnancy went beautifully. I gave birth to a healthy boy in July, 1993.

Unfortunately, after the birth of my son, I experienced severe post-partum depression. Jeff was wonderfully supportive. My family rallied behind us. A huge part of my anxiety and depression was our financial state. Jeff is an accountant who deals with millions of dollars every day. Too bad he couldn't keep our finances in order. I don't claim complete innocence, but he is basically responsible for putting us thousands of dollars in debt. My brother helped bail us out of some of our debt, which helped a great deal in my recovery. It took about two years of therapy and meds to fully overcome that episode.

When Steven, our son, was three months old, we took a trip to Florida to visit Jeff's parents. While driving in the car one night, Jeff pointed out a bar called the Copacabana. As we drove past he said, "You know that's a gay bar." Half kidding I asked him if he'd ever been there. I was more than a little surprised when he answered, "yes." I was even more taken aback by his next comment:

"You know, it never really goes away." I asked him what never goes away. He said, "the gay feelings." I told him that

that was a hell of a thing to say to a person going through a severe depressive episode. He just brushed it off and assured me that he was very happy in our marriage. In the state I was in, I was just as glad to let that go. Little did I know it would constantly come back to haunt me.

A few years passed, and our son grew thrived. When he was four years old, I found out that I was once again pregnant, this time with a little girl. My daughter was born in October, 1998. She's been a firecracker since conception! So, we had our "perfect" little family: a son a daughter, even a dog! We were even able to finally buy a house, after living in a two-bedroom apartment for ten years.

My son started to play soccer the summer he turned 5. He didn't exactly love the game and he wanted to quit. We told him the usual parent thing: "finish out the season and you don't have to sign up again next year if you don't want to." Jeff and I were talking about Steven's lack of interest in sports. He made another comment: "I just don't want him to grow up to be like me." "What do you mean, 'like you'? I asked. His answer: "you know."

At that point I decided I'd had enough. This topic came up sporadically throughout our marriage, and each time it was shoved under the rug. This time, I told Jeff that it's time he gets to the bottom of his feelings. He had to go into counseling to figure this all out. He agreed to see my friend, Susan, who had been my counselor for a few years. I knew her very well, as her kids participated in a theatre troupe that I directed.

After Jeff had seen Susan a few times, they decided it was time for the three of us to meet together. That was a meeting I will NEVER forget. All along, I believed that Jeff had never had any experiences with men. I felt that if he just tried it once, maybe he'd know for sure where his preferences lie. Well, that night I found out way more information than I could have ever anticipated. First, he told me that he had had sex with several men before he met me. Then he told me that he started having "encounters" from three months into our marriage. The first encounter happened while he was in the men's room at the college where we were working on a show together. It was the Wizard of Oz. He went to the men's room, met a guy; they "pleasured" each other, and then he returned to me, acting like the loving newlywed.

The second encounter he confessed to was while walking our dog, some guy stopped him and asked for directions. They gave each other a look, and he jumped into the guy's car, where they proceeded to pleasure each other.

My head was spinning. I really didn't think I was going to be able to survive this. In fact, suicidal thoughts were running rampant through my head. Then my friend helped me to bug my computer.

Over the next several months, I found out about so many of his indiscretions, it was mind-boggling. I learned that he had visited bathhouses during his business trips to Dallas. I learned that he had visited bathhouses during trips to Florida to visit his parents. He was Instant Messaging a friend of his, giving him detailed accounts of his antics. He also made me sound like the albatross around his neck. Each time I found something new I felt like another knife was thrust into my heart.

During one trip to Florida to visit his parents (who were quite elderly) he took our son with him. I told him before he left that I didn't want him disappearing during the night and leaving Steven alone with his parents. If Steven woke up, he wouldn't know where his dad was, and neither would his grandparents. Jeff's answer: "Point taken." Well, guess what? He DID leave Steven alone with his parents in the middle of the night. He went to a bathhouse, picked up a guy and went with this guy to his hotel room. I WAS LIVID!!! He was totally baffled when I confronted him. He had no idea how I got my information. That part was fun! I told him it didn't matter how I knew, the fact was that I did know. It didn't stop him from continuing to sow his oats.

One day, I asked him if he remembered his first time with a man. He didn't want to answer me at first. I pointed out the fact that there really wasn't anything left for me to find out. I certainly didn't think he could shock me anymore than he had. WRONG! He told me the first man he had ever had sex with was his brother. I thought I was going to be sick. Not only had they had sex, they had sex more than once. In fact they had sex several times. That was way more information than I ever thought I could handle. And, of course, I was sworn to secrecy. It's not easy being the "keeper of the secret." To this day, whenever anyone talks about what a great guy his brother is, I cringe. His wife is a nasty, malicious, instigator, and everyone wonders how such a nice guy could end up with her. She walks all over him. In fact, they're a perfect match: he needs someone to think for him, and she needs to dominate someone.

I could write an entire book about the "evil sister-in-law" but I won't waste my time. I will say, however, that when Jeff told his brother and her the truth about our separation, she went and told just about everyone she knew. She also told her then thirteen-year-old daughter about "Uncle Jeff being gay." My niece the followed her mother's lead, and told everyone SHE knew. That, by the way, included several kids who went to the school where I teach. Because of them, we had to tell our kids, especially our son, the truth before someone else did.

I took our daughter out to the movies one day last summer, leaving Jeff alone with Steven to talk. He told him that daddy is gay. When Steven said he wasn't sure what that meant, Jeff explained that daddy would rather be with men than with women. He also explained that because of this, mommy and daddy could never get back together. Of course Steven cried at that realization, but Jeff reassured him that he would be around a lot (just like he had been already) and that mommy and daddy are still a team where he and Samantha were concerned. When I got home, things were pretty calm. Steven had settled down from his meltdown.

When Jeff went home that night, I got all of the questions that were pressing on Steven's mind. The first one: "did daddy know he was gay when he married you?" When I answered truthfully that he did, Steven wanted to know why he married me. I tried to explain that daddy thought his love for me could over-power his need for sex with men. I also explained that at the time daddy and I met, being gay was still pretty taboo.

He then wanted to know why, if daddy still loves me, couldn't we stay married. I told Steven about monogamy and what marriage means. I also told him that I couldn't live with daddy knowing he's having sex with other people. Then it hit Steven: "Was daddy having sex with men while you two were married?" Once again, I was honest. The hardest part was trying to convince Steven that it didn't make daddy a bad person. He just is what he is and he can't fight it. I would never tell Steven that, at that time, I thought of his father as lower than dirt!

During our talk, Steven started to cry again. He asked me if it were true that daddy would never be living with us again. Samantha walked into the room just in time to hear me say, "I'm sorry, Steven, but daddy will NOT be moving back in." That's all she had to hear. "Daddy's not ever coming back? Why won't you let him?" OUCH! Now I had her crying in one arm, him crying in the other and I was sobbing in the middle. I called Jeff and thanked him for once again creating a mess for me to clean up. He offered to come over, but I told him, "No thank you; you've done enough." It took some time to calm the two of them down. Then I had to make Samantha understand that it's not that I won't LET daddy come back; daddy just can't come back. I wanted to tell her he was a sick, twisted, lying son-of-a-bitch, but you really can't say that to a five-year-old. So, instead, I told her he had to be on his own to figure out what he needed for his own life. And, of course, we talked about how she has two houses now.

We also discussed how luck the two of them were because many children have parents who separate, divorce and hate each other. That's not the case with us. Jeff and I get along very well. I often refer to us as "Will and Trace." We do a variety of activities together, including membership in an adult-child bowling league. We take trips together. Jeff is included in

STRAIGHT WIVES: SHATTERED LIVES

most of my family events. I choose not to be involved in too many of his family events, mainly because I don't want to have to deal with my sister-in-law. I do, however, visit his mother and call her a few times a month.

It's been two-and-a-half years since I found out how busy my husband had been during our marriage. Am I over it? I don't think I'll ever completely be over it, but I'm doing so much better now. I no longer try to plot ways to kill myself. I get involved in activities that do not include him. Most importantly, I've held onto my sense of humor. Among my friends and family, Jeff is the butt of so many jokes (no pun intended). I've decided that I'd rather laugh than cry. I'm still not really interested in pursuing new relationships right now. I'd like to get my act together first. Losing weight and organizing my house are on the top of the list. I just need to get myself motivated enough to actually do that.

My kids are thriving. They're both doing extremely well in school. He's very involved in music, and she's a member of the "Brownies." Both of them perform regularly with my theatre troupe. My son's social skills have greatly improved. They're very well behaved and happy. What more can a parent ask for?

Would I have liked to see my life turn out differently? Of course I would. But I finally learned that I could survive without Jeff living here. I still feel cheated in many ways, but I also feel incredibly blessed to have Steven and Samantha. They are my reason for getting up in the morning. Even though Jeff has caused me so much pain and resentment, he gave me the gift of my children. Because of that, I'm able to forgive him (to a point) and move on with my life.

There are some unanswered questions regarding my marriage and separation that I'd like to address now.

First of all, it took about six months from the time I learned of most of Jeff's "indiscretions" for me to ask him to move out. We had a friend who had just bought a house and was giving up an apartment that was perfect for him. It's a studio, about a mile from my house, and very reasonable rent. I told Jeff I thought he should take the apartment. "I don't get a say in this?" he asked me. My reply was simple: "You had plenty of 'say' throughout our entire marriage. I just didn't know it." You see, Jeff is not used to having to take the responsibility for his actions. Now, not only was he caught, but also he couldn't get himself out of it. I knew there was no way I could continue to live with him.

I first noticed our sex-life beginning to deteriorate after the birth of our son. Initially, I chalked it up to "baby exhaustion" and the overwhelming responsibility that goes with parenting. After our son turned two, our physical relationship continued to go downhill. Jeff would force himself to stay up on the couch watching television instead of coming to bed. I was beginning to think that there was something wrong with me: (I'm too fat; I'm not attractive, etc.). At all times, that confession was in the back of my mind: "it never really goes away."

We got "back on track" for a while, until I got pregnant with our daughter. That pregnancy was a little more difficult; a great deal of morning sickness (more like all day sickness)! When she was born, Jeff continued to lose interest in me. Our physical contact was infrequent, at best. It's one thing to be alone and feel lonely, but to have someone lying next to you, who has no interest in you, is the absolute loneliest feeling there is. Once again, I turned it on myself. I had gained a lot of weight, and I was becoming more miserable about it. Jeff swore it had nothing to do with me, but when your own husband doesn't want to come near you, what are you supposed to think?

Story 9: My Life, My Children and Moving On, Learning to Love Yourself". By Vivian

There I was in high school. Everyone was having fun and I was not. My childhood had not been a great one. My parents never got along. I didn't find out until later in life that our family life was not a typical one. My mother was over protective. My family was dysfunctional as I have now figured out. I did not have many friends. I was overweight as a child and now I had lost weight. I was not socially smart. I was not outgoing. I had never had a boyfriend. I had school phobia in middle school. I was still having problems with that. I always felt like I never belonged. Like I was the outsider looking in. Then I met my future husband. He was 18 and owned his own business, I was 15½ and in the 10th grade. I was business smart and he liked that. He gave me all kinds of attention. He listened to me. He showed me things I never knew about, things that were not in my world. He never pushed me into doing anything stupid or wrong. He had good morals and values. We had fun together. My life turned from boring and dull into spectacular and fabulous. I had something to look forward to everyday.

I graduated high school a year early at 16 1/2. Right after that we got engaged. Thinking back now, what was I thinking? I knew I was not going to get married right away, I wanted to go to college. He really pushed the issue about getting engaged, as I remember it. I figured I could always back out if things changed. I thought I had a really good guy and why loose him. My family thought at the time it was wrong and I that had never really dated anyone else. They thought maybe we should cool it for a while and see how we both feel. I did not want to loose him, so I went along and got engaged.

I ended up going to work for my family's business out of high school and going to college at the same time. His family sold their home and he ended up having no place to live. My mother offered for him to come live with my family. He was supposed to be staying in another room, he ended up staying in my room in his own bed. Looking back as a mother myself now, I can't believe my mother allowed that in her home. What was she thinking? I was almost 17. That basically decided that was going to be it for me. He quickly became part of our family. My family and my extended family had come to love him. He was Mr. Personality. He did and said all the right things. My younger brother had an older brother to look up to. My parents had another son. He ended up coming to work for the family business.

It was a very awkward living situation that I had. Back then, you did not live together unmarried. A few years later, I wanted to get married. My father said not until I finished college. So I said "Fine, I quit". I figured I was going to work for the family business forever anyway. I was so naive back then. My ex even wanted to convert to my religion (I never asked), so I could have the wedding of my dreams and when the children came, we would all be the same religion. My family was thrilled was his decision, another right move on his part. We married, I was 19 and he was 22.

The first year was good. I had a little trouble adjusting to some things. Remember my mother was over protective. I never cooked, did laundry and I only had to help with dinner. He showed me how. I had never made a whole dinner before. I mean cooking one. Little by little, working together, everything fell into place. We had our home, we had our life and we were happy. As far as I knew sexually, (I had no previous experience) everything was fine. We both were working at the family business. A year after we were married, I found out I could not have children. He was so kind and caring about it. I was devastated. "So, we will adopt" he said. It was never a heartbreaker for him. "We will work it out," he said.

His previous business got us involved with rental properties. We did that on the side. We did everything together. We rehabbed those properties together. He taught me how to do that kind of work too. Some of the work we learned how to do together. That was our hobby. We made good money doing it. We always worked so well together. It was like he was the pilot and I was the co-pilot. It was always a partnership. We were best friends. Life was good.

We had decided after about 4 years of marriage to start a family. It was not easy back then when you wanted to adopt. In 1984, we were blessed with a beautiful baby girl. I thought God was giving me the ultimate gift—a newborn baby. How lucky was I? People try to get a child and can't and I have a new baby? This child was so precious to me. I was forever grateful for this chance to be a mother. I wanted to be the best mother and give this child the best life. I felt this child had come to me for a reason. My ex was the doting father. He had the greatest relationship with her. She just loved her dad. He would go and do things with her, just the two of them. They had a special relationship. I was extremely lucky. I got to bring her to work with me until she was 18 months old. My ex worked with me, no more family business. We still got a long good at work. We got to see everything and didn't miss a thing. I thought my life was just perfect now.

In 1986, we opened our own business. 50-50 partnership, just like everything else we had done. Our life was on track. We were working towards a goal. We had our little family and we did everything together and life was good. In 1988, my ex decided we needed a bigger home. I was not so sure. He pushed for it. He found a lot and we built his dream home. It was big and overwhelming. We moved in early 1989. That spring we got a call and were blessed with a newborn son. I had given up on getting another child, but another newborn. I thought this couldn't be. This just does not happen. My ex was ecstatic. His dream was always to have a son. We had our family all set. This was what we had planned. God had blessed us like I could never have imagined.

That summer my husband was in an accident. He shattered a bone in his leg in the afternoon. We did not realize it until later that evening when he was in severe pain and starting going into shock. He needed immediate surgery. After that surgery, he was never the same man I married. During the surgery, they did nerve damage to his other leg. He had trouble walking. He was just miserable. He had a reaction to the drugs they gave him after the surgery. He came home from the hospital and was the most demanding and nasty person you could ever imagine. I thought ok, this is when in the marriage vows they say for better or worse, and this is the worse. I became superwoman. I had a baby under 6 months old who was with me 24 hours a day including coming to work with me, a first grader, a business to run, this huge house to take care of, and a husband that was cranky, miserable and no help to me at all. In fact, he was like a third child to me.

After this, he could get up and around on crutches. He started hanging out with this guy that ended up being on the payroll at work. My husband did not work for over six months. This employee would take my husband around because my husband could not drive. Well, it did not end there. They would go hunting and fishing which my husband never did before on work time. I finally put my foot down and said either he goes or I go. I found out later, he was the first one. I had no idea. This man was married, but as I know now, so what!

A few months went by and he was better. He started hanging around with another guy that was in his early 20's that was obviously gay. My husband said they were just friends. He lived at home with his parents. I found it very odd but didn't think much of it because my husband was not or so I thought. One night I was very sick and went to bed early, and put the kids to bed too. A voice woke me up in the middle of the night, telling me to go downstairs. Finally, I got up and went downstairs. As I walked across the family room, I saw in the reflection of the window someone pulling up his pants. I told my husband what I saw. He said, "You are obviously tired, you could not have seen that, we are watching movies." I know what I saw. I had not touched him since the surgery because of his pain. Well now I was not going to touch him anymore or ever again. He was already sleeping in the spare room. I guess that's why he never wanted to come back to the master bedroom. I was in denial. I said this can't be. I filed it but could not comprehend it. I was in shock, disbelief, horror and I was so overworked, overtired and overwhelmed from everything else, I just let it go.

Over the next several years, he would have a "friend" for a while and then not for months at a time. I can't even remember them all. Some would show up at work. He would go out to lunch with them or whatever they were doing. Sometimes he would go out at night; sometimes he would not for long periods of time. Sometimes he would not work for long periods of time and sometimes he would work. With the work, it was more not working then working. I was running everything for the most part. I didn't know when he would come around to help.

He would be there sometimes to help and most times not. He would not pick up a gallon of milk for me at the store if we needed it. I was working 52 hours a week and running the children to school and picking them up at after school care by myself. I was taking them to doctor's appointments. If they were sick, it was my problem. I was basically alone in everything. I was like a robot. When he felt like it, he would pop in and help. That was the last 10 years of my marriage. Some of that time, I can't even remember what happened—it is blocked from my memory. I was trapped at work all day and then at home with the children every night. I was married but very alone.

I was living in hell. I was depressed. I gained lots of weight. There was no one to talk to, no where to turn to. I could not even talk to my family. I was embarrassed, ashamed and humiliated. He made the outside world think our life was wonderful. We would act like father of the year when necessary, my daughter knew better. He would act like husband of the year when he had his wonderful holiday parties that he would throw. My family thought I was living in wonderland. People were actually jealous of my life and told me so. If they only knew.

Little did they know the pain I was suffering inside of me. I too put on a good show when I had to. Most nights, I went home and cried myself to sleep. Only a few people knew I was really hurting and they were too afraid to ask me why. I realized it would only be time before he found "the one" and then something would have to change.

Eight years ago he found "the one." His behavior towards me got worse. He was verbally and emotionally abusive. I started to go to counseling. The counselor told me he had a Narcissist Personality Disorder. My husband even tried to stop me from going to counseling. He was working me pretty good. He had me believing I could not leave, that I could not survive without him and no one would ever want me. The counseling really helped get my mind clear.

My husband then started going out in public with his "friend". That's when my weight really went up. They were shopping, dining and going to movies. He was buying him gifts and even a leather couch for him on our credit cards. I had people doing business with us asking "who is that man out with your husband all the time?" They were together constantly. My husband could not work if his "friend" had the day off from work. If this man called anytime day or night, my husband would jump. The children and I became second class citizens to him. After a while, the two lovers could not be without each other overnight. He was sneaking this man into our home and sleeping with him in the spare bedroom. He had me lying to everyone including his parents as to what was going on. I said, "Enough. I do not want this man sleeping in our home." So, my husband didn't sleep at our house anymore. He would sneak back home early in the morning and say he got home late the night before. Things were getting really bad.

I finally got the courage to confront him. I wrote it all down first, everything that was going on. I made him read that. He would not admit to anything. I said I do not care anymore. He was hyperventilating so badly. He finally said it. Yes, I am with another man. He was trying to tell me we could stay married and not loose everything. He was offering me all different kinds of scenarios. I said, "I want a divorce. Period. I am not going to stay married to you. I gave you 24 good years of my life. I want my own life. I have sacrificed and lied enough for you. I have been a prisoner all these last 10 years."

I thought I stayed for my children so they could a have their family and their home a little longer. I was worried that I would walk away with nothing, no car, no health insurance and no job. He fought me only on the custody of the children and the child support. He didn't want to pay anything and he wanted our son to live with him. He fought me hard on that. He physically threatened me, but I could not prove it. My son wanted to live with him. I gave up the fight. I said my son will go live with him and it will either work out great which will be good for my son or they will crash and burn and my son will be back with me. He defaulted after I served him.

I got my divorced 9 months later. It cost me $7000 because of the business. He paid a lawyer $75 to check it over. He later told me he was talking to other gay fathers about how to do all of this. They told him never admit you are gay. He had coaching the whole time while I was suffering. Talk about injustices.

A year after my divorce, I was diagnosed with Lupus. Since then I have also gotten Fibromyalgia, Raynauds and Sjogrens Syndrome. I am tired a lot, and my muscles ache and really have to pace myself. Most mornings I have to push myself to get up and go to work. Some days I am really energetic. It is a day to day thing for me now. Now, even going grocery shopping can be a chore.

Things after that only got worse. Three years ago, I lost the home I bought after the divorce. I am now living in an apartment. I am driving an old car. About six months ago, I had to go bankrupt due to the debt that was left when my divorce lawyer did not properly clear the joint debt that we had left over from the divorce.

Yes, I am still working with him. The business has survived all this. The business is doing well. You ask, why I am still working with him? Well, where can I work that I can call in late if I am exhausted and want to sleep in? I can also take a power nap in the afternoon if I need it. I can leave to go to the many doctors' appointments I have. I can take my children to the doctors when they need to go to. Right now, I have two standing appointments that I go to every week, and no employer would put up with that. How does he act at work? Some days he is very nice and will tell me I am over doing it; other days he is back to what he was like when we were married. He has been working hard lately and has been verbally abusive again about how I am working. He feels I am not pulling my weight at work. I am at a place mentally where I do not let it bother me as much. When the summer comes, it will be hard again for me as he won't want to work at all. He will want to be out on his boat.

I think I have hit the bottom now, and there is no place to go but up. The good news is I have lost over 100 pounds but still have some more to go. I have learned some tough lessons that might help someone else. Looking back, my children would have been better off if I had gotten out sooner. I wish I had. I didn't have the strength, energy or support to do it. Ask for help. My daughter at 21 is still feeling the effects of all of this. She will never forget the special relationship she had with her father previous to all this, that she so misses. She could not go on to college, which she is now regretting. She will go back and do it I keep telling her she can. She still needs counseling, as do all of us to deal with what happened to us. My son was 10 when we divorced. It finally hit him when he was around 14-15.

My children jump at any crumb now that their father will throw them. He is so busy with his boyfriend; he has little to no time for his children. He promises to do things but never follows through. He seems to have no patience for them anymore. He does not do the things other fathers do with their sons and their daughters. It is a shame. We were so blessed to have these wonderful children. I never wanted them to come from a divorced home which is another reason I tried to stay.

I wonder still to this day if he knew about himself this when we adopted these beautiful children. If so, what a sin he committed. I am so thankful for the chance to be a mother for these beautiful children I have. They are the ones that got me through this divorce. Without them, my life would be worthless. I am so sorry for all they had to go through for his mistakes.

My ex took away our family, our life as we knew it, my dreams, my self-esteem and the self-esteem of my children, our home, my credit, and my being able to trust people. All I ever wanted was a loving husband, happy and healthy children, a good life and to be happy. I do not care about the material things—they are worth nothing. Your sense of your own self and how others you love are being treated is the most important thing. I was reduced to believe I was worth nothing, meant nothing, had nothing to offer and no one else would want me either. I lost my sense of self so bad that I let myself gain well over 100lbs.

There are years I can't even remember what happened. My memory is gone. My children lost part of their childhood and their innocence. I have lost those years for both my children and me, and we cannot get those back. I wish I had done something much sooner. I will have to live with this forever. No one deserves to be treated that way, especially when you have done nothing except marry a man that you didn't know was gay. While he is trying to figure out his life, he is ruining yours. You need to get help, get support and get out. Do it for yourself, do it for your children.

Story 10 - My Story by Jean

It has been fourteen months since I left my home of twenty years. In July of 2005 I was divorced. Some days it feels like it was yesterday that my world imploded and my life ended, as I knew it. I long to be back with my family unit. Yet that family unit was shattered and no longer exists. On a good day, when I feel good about my life and my successes, I feel like it has been years since I left and the pain is behind me. Yet I am still on a roller coaster ride emotionally feeling like I have a bi-polar personality disorder.

I left a day before our eighteenth wedding anniversary, which was Valentine's Day. I took my piano, violin, one half of the furnishings, my paintings, portfolios and the family dog, Bernice. I left behind my son who was a senior in high school, my four kitties, the other one-half of the furnishings, and my gay husband who broke my heart with his deception. Not having a choice, I had to leave to save my life and my sanity. Our home was falling down literally because my builder husband would not repair and replace structural damages. Our bedroom, after six years was still being refurbished. The window treatment on the sliding glass door was a king sized bed sheet and the smaller window had a blanket covering it while a screwdriver held back the blanket on sunny days. The last year, I was sleeping in a spare bedroom that had mold on the walls and a closet door hanging off the doorframe. I tried to cover the neglect with my paintings but I could not cover up the abuse I was experiencing.

My husband came from a wealthy New England family, and the house he grew up in was a historical landmark, where he lived before he bought our house. I, on the other hand, came from a mid-western middle class family where both parents worked. Before our marriage, I owned four homes and left behind my condo on the bay in San Francisco to move to Connecticut to marry this man. We were in our 30s when we married. I had moved prior to meeting him, in one decade,

25,000 miles expanding my Design Career, while he moved 25 miles in that same decade. We laughed about how much I had moved and how little he had. Little did I know how truly different we were.

I believe there was love in the beginning and our son was conceived in that love. However, as time went on that love changed and died. My husband had an agenda to get rid of me. Part of that agenda was not to repair the house so the value of the house would be much less than the market allotted. Since I was in Massage Therapy school, working toward a new career, to get us out of financial debt, I could not even afford to purchase the house let alone fix it. I asked my husband to move out until the divorce was final. He refused and told me we needed to "suck it up" and live together as if nothing had happened. Renting an apartment was my only option. Six months after I moved out I graduated, passed my national MT boards and got divorced.

Life got worse before it got better. A week after the divorce was final our family cat Charlotte died in my arms. She became angry after I left the house, then became ill and was suffering from a kidney disease. Two weeks later, my son and his friends were caught smashing mailboxes, a rural pass time for bored teenagers. My son called me at 4 AM one morning to get him out of jail. The boys made restitution and a month later, in the same courthouse that the divorce was finalized, the charges were dropped.

In September 2005, my son went to college and I was homeless. The apartment house I was renting was sold and my move to Texas was cancelled. So, my things went into storage and I moved back and forth between two friends' homes every three days for one long month. My ex-husband told me to get a seasonal rental when I told him I was homeless. That was all he said. When I found out that he had not wanted to be married for many years nor had he loved me, I asked him, "When did you stop loving me"? He responded by saying that it wasn't so much when he stopped loving me but that it did not work any longer. That was all he said. I did not realize at that time that he was gay. I knew he had a one time sexual experience with a man before we were married, but he told me it was in his past, he had loved Dan but now he loved me. I believed him yet I wondered how he could love this man if it was only a one-time experience.

Throughout the years, when we entertained inviting friends and family, his ex-lover would show up. We went to all of Dan's art shows while my husband supported him emotionally. Yet he could not support my art career emotionally.

Before I filed for divorce a mutual friend spilled the beans and told me Dan had loved my husband all of our married years and that they had a major relationship prior to our marriage. Dan was openly gay and did not hide his gender choice. It was not a one-time experiment as I was told or did I only hear that it was a one-time experiment because that was what I wanted to hear. My husband said he was now his friend and nothing more. I believed him. When I asked him to talk to me, he would say that I had married a quiet man. He was always unavailable emotionally and eventually shut me out totally. He was abusive mentally and psychologically by ignoring me for years and then shutting me out of our bedroom that last year. After we discussed getting divorce I realized he was a Passive Aggressive personality. Actually, I was clueless and didn't know how badly he was abusing me. I was too busy keeping the family together and not seeing what was truly happening.

Then after putting the pieces together and letting go of the illusion I had created, I realized what he meant by "it didn't work any longer". The DECEPTION didn't work any longer. He was always homosexual acting as a heterosexual, and that was the deception. When I asked him if he was ever attracted to men in our eighteen years of marriage, he smiled and raised his eyebrows, as to say of course, that is a ridiculous question and what else have you uncovered. However when I started talking about his passive aggressive personality, he dismissed me.

This whole tragedy hit me like a ton of bricks. My gay x-husband NEVER has called to see how I am doing, to find out where I am living and if I am working. He just dismissed me from his life after twenty years, like I had died and left the planet. I feel that he is cold-blooded and heartless yet maybe he is finally being himself, and that is fearful. Fearful of me and what I represent—and that is a heterosexual relationship. If only I could remove the memories of him from my mind and keep my son's childhood and animals intact as sweet memories.

I do Hospice work and have written a book about the transitional experience called "Their Last Painting, Stories of Life That Will Rock Your Heart". It is about unconditional love being eternal. Many people have died in my arms including my parents and the pain from losing them is huge. But not as huge as having someone who you loved and thought loved you dismiss you from his life as if you were dead. There is no communication unless it involves something about our son and then it is brief. Unconditional Love is eternal IF it is there to begin with and not an illusion that was created.

My book will soon be published. I have two positions as a Massage Therapist in my new career and I tutor art students. My son calls once a week and visits occasionally. I am planning to move back to California where I lived before I was married, and this is a positive plan. Since I had to take my dog, Bernice, back to the family house because she had Separation Anxiety and Inflammatory Bowel Disease, I now have a Maine Coon cat named Isaac. He takes away 50% of my loneliness. Yet every day is a struggle even though I am moving forward into the possibilities that life has to offer. Living alone, again suddenly, after twenty years of nurturing and caring for a family, is not fun.

This divorce is final as our relationship is finally over. Hearing love songs on the radio upset me because I realize our love and marriage was fraudulent. We were like oil and water, they don't mix, and neither did we. We looked at life differently and our energy did not blend. My sexuality, self-worth and heart are damaged. I did not pay attention to the red flags and some days I still can not believe my life, as a family unit, is over.

Letting go is my only option—letting go of everyone and only those who are supposed to return will. It is a long healing process with roadblocks along the way but I know creating a new life will heal me totally someday. In creating that new life I will trust myself first; trusting my intuition is the way to happiness and if I do not know what to do I will do nothing. I will follow my Spirit without hesitation, living with passion, unconditional love and compassion. For now when my heart hurts and loneliness consumes me I will pick myself up while knowing this will pass too and focus on my truth, my Hospice work and my kitty who is unconditional love.

Story 11: And Then There Was One by Jan K.

I could not tell you my story without first telling you a brief history of where I have been. I grew up in a small rural community, the eldest of four children. My father was a successful supervisor of many stores and out of town a lot. I craved my father's attention, but he would sometimes yell a lot. He was made to bear the major portion of the discipline when he would get back into town. He would sometimes hit the boys, but not the girls, and I was scared to death when this happened.

Church was the focal point of the day. I was drenched in religious camaraderie and ethics. Living in a small rural area gave you little access to girl friends, so I had boys that were friends. Our graduating class boasted a whopping ninety-seven and of those ninety-seven almost seven were or had homosexual leanings. Three of those seven were my best friends. The class ahead and two behind mine also boasted a number of gay males. This number was high because there happened to be a married gay man who preyed on young males living in our area. He was finally arrested and jailed, but not before many young males were introduced to the lifestyle. My very best male gay friend once told me that, "I was the only one that could turn him straight." I was flattered.

I met and married my first husband before I was out of college. I thought I could change him. He was jealous, self-absorbed in getting ahead and very much old-school. He was young also, and trying to make his way in the business echelon. He didn't have time for me. I discovered I was pregnant and it was not going well. Something was wrong! I started my first teaching assignment and would double over with pain and gushing amniotic fluid. No one was helping me and I went about seeking a new doctor. I met this new gynecologist who put his hands between my legs the morning I had my D & C and said, "It's going to be all right, I will take care of you." I woke up to find my husband at work, the "good" doctor by my bedside and a new basement being dug for our new home. It was the date of our third anniversary.

The doctor would call often to see how I was doing. He invited himself over on several occasions and I told him, "No!" When I went in for my follow-up exam he paid so much attention to me and treated me so kindly that eventually I gave in. This began a two-and-a-half year affair with a man that was five years younger than my father.

I look back on this time and all I can say is that I felt sorry for Monica Lewinski. It was a similar situation. This doctor was an abusive man, who took advantage of a young woman when she was most vulnerable. He used his position, money and authority. I was beside myself with grief, and guilt. My marriage was over, I had to change teaching assignments, my new boss was horrid and I was on Valium, prescribed by the doctor, to calm myself down.

Enter my current, soon-to-be ex husband, Chas. We worked in the same building. He was, I thought, my God sent soul mate. He was kind, thoughtful, attentive to a point, but self-centered. On our first date, he asked my "standing with the Lord." Was I a Christian? I didn't realize, but, because of my past, and the situation I had just come out of, I was ripe for the "picking." I overlooked many of the signs. His mother and grandmother were the focus of his life. If it didn't fit his time line or his desires, then it didn't fly.

He said he coached so people wouldn't questions his orientation, because of the subject he taught. His apartment was like no males I had ever seen, immaculate, decorated to the nines; he was almost obsessive/compulsive about himself and his environment. His first marriage ended because of several conditions, but the biggest was that Chas thought his first wife was a lesbian; she was, and is. Chas didn't push for sex, which was a relief. The whole previous relationship was about sex, and nothing else. I was thirsting for a social, religious relationship, and I got it.

Sex with Chas was ho-hum, but I figured it was just that I had had an affair with a gynecologist. I thought it would get better or more frequent. NO WAY! Sex never got better, no sex two days in a row, no cuddling afterward, just jump up and wash up, and no repetitive love making. Oral sex began and ended on the night we got married. I lost a baby soon after we were married, my second now. This led to the "no sex ban" once I did conceive, "Might hurt the baby!"

Chas would tell you that we drifted apart and he started to feel this separation of our lives into separated people living in the same house shortly after our second child. He has told me that his jealousy of the children and the time I spent with them also began at this time. I really felt it after the birth of our third child and his vasectomy. Silly me, I thought or read somewhere that the sperm build up and the man has an urge to release. I thought the vasectomy killed his urge for sex.

I was teaching, parenting three children, and running a business he and I had started. I was so exhausted I didn't care that we didn't have sex that often. He was involved with his church and his people there, and Chas said that he was so socially exhausted from people always wanting his time, that we gave up all friends and social engagements.

To get away from people and their demands he found this favorite spot at the beach to go and relax. Sometimes he would take the children and me along, but he would walk a mile by himself to a private area where he could sunbathe privately. He said there was nothing wrong with this. It was just his way of enjoying the out of doors and a form of release.

Chas always had money for what he wanted. They say that marriages end over sex and money. Well, that is certainly true in my case! He would never budget. He had his money and I had mine. When the kids reached school age, Chas pretty much gave full responsibility for their education expenses, sport outings, lessons and clothing to me. He started going to the health club, to preserve his physique and get over his "mid-life crisis", in the early morning and that pretty much killed any sex life we had left. He had every excuse in the book. Headache, backache, groin ache, too much sun, and etc. He said that he wanted me to be the aggressor, but how much turn down can you take? How can you start something when the man that is supposed to love you, turns his back. There is no affection, no romance, no, "I love you just because."

When our eldest went away to college, Chas would go into her bedroom to sleep after midnight. This way the other kids wouldn't know that he hadn't slept with me. He would leave for the health club before they got up. He said it was because I breathed too deeply or snored and it kept him awake. I was so alone. I wanted to be touched, held, romanced; loved. I got so desperate that when Chas went away on his first of many excursions to Vegas I bought a new mattress. I thought maybe he didn't want sex because the bed squeaked. That didn't help either!

One day a teacher, Para-pro came in and gave me a business card from "someone I used to know." I e-mailed this someone; it was my first husband. We e-mailed, he was divorced again and we decided to meet. He actually looked me in the eye and said, "How are you?" I replied "alright." He knew I was lying. He was upbeat, alive and actually listened to me talk. Someone actually cared that I was alive. One thing led to another and my kids found my e-mails to my first husband, my son found the web sites of his father, his father denied their existence; he still denies their existence. My therapist suggested I write Chas a letter saying how I felt and expressing my suspicions about his sexuality. Explosions hit like the Fourth of July! My kids insisted on a divorce. I was the horrible person that had hurt their father, my son hated his dad and me, and after ten months of tension and discontent, Chas moved out.

We have tried therapy, or rather I have; there is nothing wrong with Chas, it was and is my entire fault. We have tried moving back in together, but you can't build a relationship in a vacuum. Chas is very passive aggressive. On the day I moved back in with him, he went golfing. He will never admit that he is gay, even though I have multiple web-sites, pictures of his lingerie and the biggest clue—no sex for years and years. He is too religious; he would never admit to his "dear" mother his preferences and his church following would be devastated. My son says that I will never break the bond that Chas has with his mother. When she is in the house there is no one else around; all of his attention is placed on her and the conversations that they have.

I go through periods of great sadness. When I read Bonnie's chapter on Limbo-wives I wept so hard I actually fell on the floor and cried and cried until I threw up. I could not understand how someone could be married for twenty-seven plus years and not love the other person. I moved into an apartment this past fall and recently I bought my own place and I moved in this past spring. I sit on the porch of my home and watch the birds, the boats and the people go by. I still find it difficult because my youngest still lives with Chas. If I want to see the children, I have to go to his house to do that. It is difficult going from being married and part of a couple, mother, wife, and companion, to being an empty nester, by myself and out of the family loop. I will persevere; I am still in therapy and at this point in time have no desire to be involved with anyone. I can find new hobbies though and new areas to get involved in. There is a difference between alone and being lonely. One of my gay male friends now said, "Stop concentrating on what might have been and isn't, and concentrate on what you could have in the future." I am still very comfortable around gay males. I think it has to do with my very early beginnings, and this is part of the reason that I am content to be just one at this time. I was one for so many years; it was just not in a home by myself. Today and for tomorrow though, it will be; And Then There Was One!

Story 12 – Susanne

We don't receive wisdom;
We must discover it for ourselves
After a journey that no one can take for us or spare us.

Marcel Provoust
French novelist
(1871 – 1922)

Everyone knows someone who reads the last page of a book first to see if she wants to read it. Somehow knowing the ending makes the investment of time more worthwhile. Wouldn't it be nice if all our stories can turn out like that? They can. Last night while I was washing dishes, the container of dish washing liquid spurted a bunch of tiny bubbles when I put it down. I realized just how incredibly happy and at peace I was to find such delight watching those bubbles move about the kitchen. How did I get to this place? I never thought it was possible.

In 1983 my husband of six years left me for one of his employees. I was devastated. We were college sweethearts. I worked while he went to dental school and after he graduated, he decided to practice in suburbia without even consulting me. I had a new job which was horrible. He then told me he never wanted to have children. We moved forward with divorce because I thought this to be true. I was very "righteous" in those days and Connecticut had what I called "no fault divorce." Since we were just starting out there was nothing to divide. He convinced me I should get out of this marriage because he was depressed and I should move on while I was still young enough to have children.

Six months later he married his hygienist and they went on to have two sons.

What does this have to do with being a straight wife with a gay husband? You have to know where you've been to decide where you are going. Enter "Gary"; a blind date, nice looking, polite, great with kids, worked for a car dealership. What's not to like? I was told statistically that I had a greater chance of being hit by lightening than remarrying and having children. Remember, this was before internet dating! We were married in 1985 and had our daughter in 1987.

After Crystal was born, I began seeing changes in him. He was present at our child's birth and said he could not make love to me any more because he saw our baby come out of my vagina. There is such a psychological condition, so I somehow was able to understand it. I had to work full time and realized that I was not going to get help with the baby, apartment, finances, emotional support, nothing. There was no reasoning with him; he just wanted to continue the same way he did before the baby was born; but life had changed.

When Crystal was three years old Gary lost his job. We couldn't afford day care and he was forced to take care of her three days a week and look for a job the other two. He was resentful and somehow felt this was *my* fault. Our love life was intermittent. I had never lost the "baby weight" and the stress was making me eat more. Crystal was in kindergarten before he decided to work again.

Gary went to work for a posh department store as the head of housekeeping. Many of the staff were openly gay and flirted with him. He used to come home and we'd laugh about it. He was slim and had a nice butt in jeans.

Who knew? He had an affair with one of female staff. I think he did it to ward off the gay staff and show them he was a "man/" The hurt and emptiness that one feels after this betrayal cannot be described in words. I blamed myself and didn't even know why.

The cliché answer was low self esteem. We went to marriage counseling and I resolved to get over this. We even separated for awhile only to find ourselves back together and miserable again. Now that Crystal was older, he had a little buddy to play with. He was a big kid with her and she idolized him. I did not want to be a "two time loser" and divorce again. I just thought I would see it through for the shake of our child.

Life was a whirl wind and I was spinning in the vortex. He lost his job in the department store because of "poor work performance". He became depressed and stayed home, to just smoke his unemployment checks away. Crystal had to stop the after school program and Gary would meet her school bus. What was he doing from 8:30 AM to 3 PM?

The INTERNET had come into being. I would call home during the day and the line would be busy all the time. Then he got wise to my questioning and would call me at work just to say "hi" and then go on line for hours.

We got a scanner for the computer and digital camera. I thought we were doing this for Crystal. Do you see where this is going? I, at the time, was not computer savvy. It took our thirteen- year-old daughter to take me down that road. She was torn between keeping her father's secret and being un-loyal to her mother. What an awful place for a kid to be put in. She showed me her father's profile which stated "bisexual, married but looking." There was a trail of gay chat rooms, web sites, and porn. She even found a picture of him naked. In those days we thought "delete" meant it was gone.

There was so much evidence, so much pain and confusion, that even upon confrontation, he denied it. It was "just a phase", "I was curious" etc. etc. I think anyone reading this story has heard this, perhaps multiple times. After one had resolved the first indiscretion, it was shocking and demeaning to be betrayed again. How much worse could it get? There weren't any more tears left. I was depleted.

Then it all began to be my fault once more. I was accused of being a domineering nag, never allowing him to be himself, to be free, to experiment, to live life to its fullest. Have you heard, "It really isn't cheating on you because it was with a guy"? All my life I had to compete with men. When I went to college, programs were still hesitant to give away a spot to a woman. We worked for less pay doing the same job. This was the last time I was going to compete with a man for the same thing, and the irony of it was that it was another man.

The thought of people being homosexual did not bother me. I saw no shame in being gay. I was actually happy but deeply hurt at the same time. The real reason behind his depression was not as he led me to believe for so many years, but his struggle with who he was. I grieved for what seemed to be an eternity. It was almost like the same stages that one goes through when you are dying, and I truly felt like I was. Disbelief, anger, bargaining, and acceptance, sometimes you slip back and forth between the first three stages trying to make sense of it all.

Now remember, I live in the land of "no fault divorce." Since he had not been working for so many years he was entitled to alimony and health insurance until he remarried. Now what were the chances of that? We did not own a home, we were in debt from all his credit card spending, there was no savings, and he did not want to leave. I couldn't afford a lawyer, but he was eligible for a free one!

It was the lowest point of my life. I was too ashamed to tell family and friends. I was just waiting for some divine intervention to make this nightmare go away. We agreed to another year of this if he didn't "date." This was non-negotiable. Within the year he would try to either cut down smoking or find a part time job. We would seek help together or alone to get through this. I agreed to not talk to him about our contract for six months. I was known to be easily taken advantaged of by his manipulative nature in the past. To be clear, I wrote up an agreement that I thought was full of love, hope, and support for him to get on his feet and be who he was born to be.

True to my word, I checked in with him in six months. His reply was. "What agreement?" I knew at that point I was dead in the water. He was also seen around town with young men in coffee shops. I went to the city courthouse and picked up a packet for a "do it yourself divorce." It referenced law books that were available at the law library. I had a dear friend who was a lawyer in the next state and she told me I would be destroyed by doing this myself.

A year to the day of our agreement as promised, I filed papers for divorce. Gary was absolutely shocked. He never thought I "had the balls" to do it. I asked him if he loved me and he said no without hesitation and surprisingly agreed it was the right thing to do. I had to tread very carefully, not to upset him during the process. I knew he could be vindictive and I would be ordered to support him "in the manner he was accustomed to" in our marriage. I worked with him to get him on disability insurance; we were able to find a prescription drug plan for his income level that was state subsidized. Our daughter was now sixteen and we were still mandated by Connecticut law to go to a parenting class or the divorce would not be possible. He said he didn't have any money for the class. As with the divorce, filing fee, sheriff charges etc. I also paid for us both to attend. He went kicking and screaming. I wanted to yell at him so badly, but I knew that would just make him bolt, and we wouldn't be able to move forward with this divorce.

Things were so uncomfortable that he moved in with his parents in a small conservative town an hour north of us. This gave me some breathing space. He came over any time he wanted to see Crystal; no rules, no restrictions, no arguments from me. He was verbally abusive and accusatory at times. My friends thought I should have gotten a restraining order. but I knew that would just ignite a volatile situation. I just had to keep believing that this was the right way to separate. We had been married nearly eighteen years. I was almost fifty and really felt that I lost a half-century of living.

I'll spare you the court room drama and a very annoyed judge who was dealing with no lawyer, no mediator, that he had to put our case at the end of the day after sending us to social services to make sure our child was cared for. It was humiliating hearing couples fighting over property, money, and their children.

It was hard to believe that we all said "I do" willingly. After making sure that Gary was adequately cared for, the judge granted our divorce. We both cried.

I am crying now as I write this. It's very sad when a marriage ends after so many attempts to save it. You cannot change a person's sexual identity and most importantly, it is not your fault, you didn't do this to him, despite what your ex-mother-in-law says you did to make him "this way"!

That happened in March, and by September, I was back in school, working full time and sharing the kitchen table with Crystal doing "homework" together. She was a senior in high school. Her grades significantly improved. Our sleeping habits, nutrition, and fitness levels were so much better, and we were having fun. Her father would show up every two weeks and swear he wasn't gay. He was even dating a few women. He asked to come back home several times; it just got easier to say no each time.

Crystal is now a commuter student at a college about an hour away.

I completed school and earned my nursing home administrator's license.

I was promoted at my present job and we did not have to move. Crystal decided that it was two years post Gary and I should try to date. I looked in the mirror and saw my mother. When did I get old? Who would want me? Who would I want at this stage of the game? I was working two jobs to help get Crystal through school and I was busy, busy, busy, filling the entire empty gaps in my life with busyness. Her father had remarried (yes a woman) whom he knew briefly, eighteen years younger than him, and had four children, none of which she had custody of. He never came out of the closet.

After kissing a few toads, I met a most wonderful man. I truly know the meaning of soul mate. Two people couldn't be more loving or compatible than us, and we ain't youngsters either! But you'd never know it to see us. We met through computer dating! Speaking of computers, Crystal's step-mother wants to know if her boyfriend used their computer. She found gay porn on it. A leopard changes his spots.

I remain,

Susanne V.

Story 13: Love Lost By: Kate L.

Who would have known that I would have met the "man" of my life on the elevator? It was late November 1988. I looked absolutely dreadful after crying in the hospital all day and night. My six year old daughter Jessica had a fever of 103.5 and had been admitted. While waiting for the elevator in my apartment complex, I saw a soldier. Having been in the military myself for several years I saw he had a rank on his uniform that I could not identify. No one else was waiting so I decided to ask him about it. We talked all the way to the 5th floor and before you knew it, we were getting off the elevator on the same floor. We each went in the opposite direction to our own apartments. I must admit I did not start talking to Aidan because he was attractive, but simply out of curiosity. It wasn't long before we were talking on the phone and went out on our first date.

Aidan was a freshman studying psychology in the local university and was also six years younger than I, but the age difference was not noticeable. I, too, was a freshman studying nursing. We enjoyed our time together and had similar views on life. We started dating on a regular basis, but our focus was on our individual studies. Aidan seemed very inexperienced in many ways when it was time for intimacy. He admitted that he hadn't dated much in high school. I thought that was odd initially being that he was a high school jock and he attracted females quite easily. I blew it off thinking he was probably always focused on his studies and his personal life came in second place. Being a single mom and a full time student I didn't have much free time left over either so I could relate to this.

After several years of dating, Aidan finally graduated and was ready to go off to his first military assignment. He made it clear to me that he had no interest in getting married and thought it best if we remained friends. My heart was saddened by the news but I understood his need to live his life freely without the responsibilities a relationship brings. I still had a year before I would finish my nursing degree and knew I too would have to move on when I returned to the military. We mailed letters back and forth for several months and then the phone calls began. It wasn't long before we were talking constantly. One Sunday night I called Aidan as usual and out of the blue he asks me to marry him. I thought he was joking and didn't give him an answer. Several weeks passed by and once again he proposed. I asked him if he was joking and sure enough he wasn't. I was ecstatic at the thought that this man wanted to marry me and be the father of my child and future children.

Things happened very quickly there after. We were married almost immediately and a few months later I was pregnant. When I told Aidan about the pregnancy he didn't seem to say much at that moment. Robert was born late November 1994. Unfortunately Aidan was away on another military assignment. Thank God for friends. Evelyn was there to hold my hand and get me through this joyous time. I don't think she knows how grateful I was to have her there by my side that day.

My son Robert met his dad when he was one month and 3 days old. Life was good with Aidan at home. We did practically everything together as a family or a couple. The love Aidan and I shared was so strong that I could never imagine life without him. During the next two years we moved three times with the military. I loved going somewhere new and learning about different people and cultures. Jessica, on the other hand, had to adapt to the many changes life threw her way. It wasn't easy for a child to move every few years leaving friends behind and having to make new best friends, again. Over the many years that passed Aidan and I grew closer and knew we could count on the other if needed. There was never a time that I felt Aidan's love for me was untrue. We always had a good and healthy sexual relationship.

After thirteen years together Aidan started to change. He had found an interest in the internet which seems to have preoccupied most of his free time. Many nights had gone by in which I found myself alone in my bed with no man to snuggle and only my thoughts that were getting the best of me. I started to doubt his love for me. He always reassured me that he was working on "something" important. The truth is I never did find out what that something important was…maybe it was better that way.

Aidan's new assignment had him traveling alone constantly. It wasn't hard to not let my fears get the best of me. I thought he had met someone on one of his trips and was cheating on me. I confronted Aidan with this assumption and once again he reassured me there was nothing to be concerned about, that I was worrying over nothing. Our relationship had hit a "snag" so to speak. I was determined to make this work no matter what. I would make every effort to prepare his favorite meals, look prettier, look sexier…what ever it took.

My efforts were useless. He kept insisting that I was imagining things. We continued normal family events as if nothing was wrong. The kids and I would go watch him play soldier,(skydiving, mountain climbing, rappelling…) whatever the event was I was there standing next to him as a loyal, faithful companion.

On my last move as a military wife, I came to where I presently live. The children and I moved first to establish a home and schools for them before the new school year. Aidan had three months left at the old assignment before he would transfer over with us. On one of his visits during those three months he came home for a weekend stating he had to return to work on Monday. I took him to the airport that Monday morning and later that evening received a call from an out of state area code which I was not familiar with. It was Aidan on the on the phone. I asked him where he was calling from and he gave me some story about calling from a military phone and that is why there was a different area code.

The following day I called Aidan's work and his boss told me he was off the rest of the week. I had no way to contact him and try to find out what was really happening, but the knot in my stomach was telling me it was not good.

Two days later he called, and when I confronted him, he told me he had been in Virginia trying out for the CIA, (Central Intelligence Agency), but didn't want to let the military know. I found this unusual but went along with it until I could get to the bottom of all this mess. Three months passed and Aidan was due home.

At first it almost seemed as though he didn't live at home yet, working 16 hours a day. He would get home very tired and all he wanted to do was sleep. Our sexual life had come to a drastic halt. The night before my life changed, Aidan showed me pictures of his travels during the three months we were apart. I immediately noticed a young man I had never seen before in one of the pictures. I asked him who the young guy was and he said "just some guy I met". As I lay in bed I thought why would he want a picture of some guy he just met?

The next day was almost like any other day, Aidan came home kissed me and told me he loved me. I was almost out the door to take Robert to his taekwondo classes when Aidan insisted on joining me. I thought it was odd but welcomed the company. When we dropped off Robert, Aidan turned around and told me those dreaded words "We need to talk". He wanted to grab a cup of coffee but I told him "if what you have to say is going to make me cry I would rather not".

He parked the car and looked down while trying to find the right words to say. I asked if we were going to get a divorce and he said "that's up to you". Lucky I was already sitting because my legs grew weary. I asked him what was happening through the tears that I was trying to fight back. Was it another woman? He answered "no" I said, is it me? Again he said, "No." I then asked him a question which I expected him to say "woman, have you lost your mind"?

Unfortunately for me when I asked if he was gay there was only silence.

It was the kind of silence that made you aware that life would never be the same again. Just thinking of that moment today still brings tears to my eyes.

My first thought was awful and to this day I am still ashamed I even thought it. I would have preferred to have heard that he passed away doing something,…anything for the military and that I would never have had to know the truth. I pushed those thoughts out of my head and hugged him while feeling pity for him.

Amazingly enough I felt sad for him that he had married and had to live a lie for so long. It wasn't until the shock wore off when I realized, what about me and my feelings in all this. Did he lie to me for fifteen years? Was any part of our life together true?

Aidan moved out immediately and it wasn't long before we were divorced. The kids learned the truth and their hearts were broken. Jessica has been in therapy and has been dealing with this matter in her own way. Robert had some counseling in school but the focus was the divorce.

Aidan is not fully "out of the closet". Only a handful of people know the truth of why we divorced. He remains in the military and everyone "assumes" that one of us was cheating on the other. So that his military career is not tainted we have now joined him in that closet. My closest friends are all military wives and none know the truth. I fear that his job will be jeopardized if the truth got out. Not to mention the humiliation my children could encounter.

It's been a little over 4 years since that day. Aidan comes over occasionally to stay in my home with the kids. I have since met his lover but am not ready yet to have him join Aidan in my home. I have moved on with my life. I have been dating David for a while and I am just taking life as it comes at me. Life has been unpredictable thus far, so I try not to think of tomorrow and focus on today. It's not easy to pull yourself together and keep going after something like this, but I must believe that tomorrow the sun will shine and it will be a brighter day.

Story 13: Clueless by Linda C.

When I was seventeen-years-old, I met a young man, Bob, at work. I worked in the front office of Waldbaums, and he was a cashier on the front end. When I first met him, I thought he was a real fool and didn't want much to do with him. My best friend Bonnie was crazy about him. After several months it was time for the annual Christmas party, and my friend Bonnie asked Bob to join her and asked me to come along with another coworker named Mike. I accepted and off we went to the holiday formal. This was a big deal for us because we had never had the chance to get dressed up in gowns and go out for the night.

As the evening progressed, I started to think that Bob was not such a bad guy after all. We started to dance, and everyone kept remarking what a great couple we made. The night ended in the wee hours, and we said our good nights and made no further commitments. After that night I couldn't get him out of my mind. When I saw him at work, he was quite shy; he would almost whisper hello and try to avoid any eye contact. Shortly after that we all went over to a mutual friend's house to hang out after work. I was determined to make him mine, so I approached him and kissed him on the lips. From that minute on, I knew he was the man that I wanted; however, he was very shy and tried to resist me.

In the months that followed we finally started to see each other on a regular basis. It was very rare that we were ever alone together because we had a lot of friends. I was devastated when another one of my friends asked him to her junior prom and he accepted. My best friend Bonnie and I waited up all night for him to return. He ended up dumping the girl, and we went to the beach the next day with some of our friends. When I told him how I felt about him, he told me he only wanted to be friends. A coworker asked me to go to the movies and I accepted because I felt as though Bob was a lost cause by now. When I returned home four hours later, he was sitting on my front porch with my mother. Wow was I flattered! So I asked him to come in and we sat up talking all night long. Finally he asked me to be his steady girlfriend and I accepted.

At this point we saw each other every day at work or at school and we were constantly together. Finally we discovered sex and he couldn't keep his hands off of me. The day didn't end unless we had sex at least once, and it didn't matter where we were, the beach, the front seat of the car, or in my parents' house, and we both loved every minute of it. This meant that we made excuses of why we didn't want to do things with our friends anymore and it became just the two of us.

I graduated high school one year before him and started my future at the local community college. I went to school full time and worked full time nights, but we still managed to be together as much as possible. A year later he graduated high school, and I attended with his very proud mom. At this point we had already been dating for three years and never talked about the future. The following Easter Sunday, after four years of dating, he asked me to marry him. I was the happiest girl in the world! We were engaged for one year and then married in May of 1979.

On our first wedding anniversary, I was eight months pregnant with our first daughter, Diana. The day was celebrated with a baby shower given by our families, and the most beautiful diamond earrings a girl could ever want from her husband. There was happiness and joy all around us because this was going to be the first grandchild for all. The baby was born a month to the day on June fourth of 1980, bringing new challenges to both of us. We really didn't have much of a clue on how to raise children; we both came from dysfunctional homes with a lot of alcoholism. To add to the misery, Bob's father showed up on our doorstep after not seeing him for many years. As the two of them made up for lost time, I was on my own pretty much to keep this baby content. There were many sleepless nights and his father visited for what seemed an eternity.

Soon I found myself pregnant again with our second child, Laura, another girl. When I brought her home from the hospital, Bob didn't even want to hold her. He kept very distant from the both of us. She was very attached to me, but I had to return to work part time nights so that her father had to babysit her and her sister while I was at work. Things went smoother and eventually he started to bond with her. I thought maybe the distance was because he didn't have a son.

We went through our ups and downs. I always tried to plan for us to get away together from our daily grind by going away for our anniversary. No matter what I would plan, the kids somehow became a part of it and we were not alone. He became very verbally abusive over the years and I always was never good enough. If we had company, I am sure that they never felt welcomed, due to the constant conflicts. We were both very busy, him with work and his love of gardening, and me with the kids, always bringing them to their activities.

On my second daughter's eighth birthday, her sister Megan was born. I can remember when I told Bob that we were expecting again, he turned as white as his starched shirt that he wore to work. Again I felt alone with another pregnancy to get through without the support that I needed. Today I know that she was a gift from above. Megan was a very busy little girl with a lot of activities such as scouting, swimming and softball. The days flew by as I volunteered and cheer leaded for her.

Suddenly, I had two daughters in college and one in middle school. Life was good. Still I always felt desperately alone. I tried hard to make everything perfect, to cook the right meal, to have the house clean, but it was never enough. I was criticized no matter what I did. I grew up in a family that did things together, so I strived to make this happen for my kids. Every summer we went away to the beach for a week with all of my extended family. This was one event that I knew I could count on. He would bury himself in a book for the week, and I would watch the kids, I didn't deserve to have a vacation.

Two years ago in May, my two youngest daughters suggested that their dad was acting weird. I asked them what they meant and they said that he was acting like a schoolgirl. The next day I called him from work and asked him if the two of us could get together to talk without the kids around. He found a babysitter for the youngest and off we went to the beach to talk. All the way there, an hour long ride, he verbally abused me. When we arrived I told him I would sit near the car until he decided he would be nice to me. We then started to walk along the boardwalk and stopped at the first bench to sit. He looked me in the eyes and told me that he was gay and had found someone else. My whole world stopped turning, and I was just numb. I think I would have coped better if he had told me he had a fatal disease. My whole body began to shake and I was speechless, spiraling into a black hole.

As the weekend progressed, we talked for hours about his new found freedom. We had sex like we never had before; he thought he may be bi-sexual. When I found out that his new mate is HIV positive, I threw him out of the bed. I went to our parish priest and poured my heart out to him, looking for some kind of an answer. Bob told me how divorce was the only answer and I begged him to stay with me. Time began to stand still for me. I didn't want to feel anything, or let anyone know about the pain I was in.

That Sunday we went to family birthday party for my nephews and just acted as if he had a date so he had to leave early. I helped him lie by saying he had to go to work. I asked him if he was going to tell the girls and he said he was going to wait until they got back in school. Adamantly I told him that they needed to be told right away. A few days later I asked the girls to be home at a certain time for a family meeting.

Late, as usual, their father walked in to tell them his news. The oldest thought that it was great, the middle one was speechless and the youngest couldn't stop crying. The one thing that was asked was that we all went on vacation together that August like we had for years before. I decided that I would take my own car in case I felt that I needed to leave. We all made it through the week with my mother-in-law in tow. He treated me very mean for the entire week, telling me to pay for my own meals, humiliating me in front of my family, and spending hours on the phone with his lover. Needless to say I haven't been on vacation since; the memories are too painful.

The divorce papers were served in September and the divorce was supposed to be uncontested. I spent many days in court as he contested everything. Thousands of dollars later we were divorced on our twenty-sixth wedding anniversary. My youngest daughter and I moved into a one bedroom apartment near her school, hoping that it would only be for a year. I have had two job losses since and am struggling to make ends meet. She visits her father on the weekends, in the beach house of his lover, and lives the good life. I know that someday she will see that her mother did her best with what she had.

Do I ever regret the path that my life has taken? No because it was a learning experience that has made me rich in many ways other than financially. Our middle daughter will be getting married next August. It gives me hope to see her so happy. I don't know what the future holds for me, it will take a long time for me to trust another man.

Story 15: Anita's Story

My name is Anita and I've been married to a gay man for the past 34 years. At the early age of 14 years old, I was trying to escape from an abusive and alcoholic family so I told my mother that I was pregnant and she never even took me to the doctor to verify it. She just signed the papers saying that i was one less mouth to feed since there were 7 siblings. We never hugged our parents or went anywhere together like other families did, and we never had enough to eat.

I met my husband when he and his father used to bring my parents home drunk from the cafe his father owned. He felt sorry for us and used to bring us food while my parents were at work and we became good friends. He was my hero and took me out of that abusive home only to cover a trail of deception and lies for the next 34 years unknown to me.

I was very naive and had no idea about the gay world that i was to be a part of. Looking back he had a friend named Terry and they were so inseparable that he even moved in with us the day we married. I'm not sure but maybe a month into our marriage we all ended up in the same bed for a threesome and my husband told Terry to teach me how to give him a blow job and terry performed on him right there in front of me. A few minutes into it they told me to go freshen up and when i came back they had locked me out and i could hear them moaning and groaning so i went into the kitchen and got a beer. Thats when the alcohol started to mellow my hurt feelings.

I had no one and nowhere to go to so i stayed and tried to wait until my husband would "get well or it would wear off." I just needed to learn how to please him, and it would just be the two of us—but that has never worked. He began to go to clubs a lot and I would find matches with the name of the clubs on them, but I was too afraid to go see what was going on.

Later in the marriage my husband brought home a co-worker and his family for a barbeque and said that I should spend time with his wife while they went out. By that time I had my oldest daughter who was 3, and the other wife had a 4 year old and a 2 month old girl. So we stayed home and took care of the kids while they use to go out a lot. i told my husband that i needed a car to get back and forth to the laundry and stores since they were hardly there. His new co-worker and wife had moved in with us by then my husband said they needed to get on their feet by staying with us a while. I agreed that it would be okay.

One night we found a sitter and decided to go to this club that they had been hanging out at and catch them with their women and confront them, but little did we know that it was a gay bar. We snuck in and we spotted our husbands on the dance floor dressed in the same color shirts and jeans. They had their shirts tied up to their breast line and were dancing in synch as two lovers would. We hurried out of there and went home in silence knowing that we had gay men as husbands, and yes, we knew they were lovers. But what could we do with children, no job, and no family to turn to? So we just drank until many months later they finally ended their affair and we all moved on to the next section of my disoriented marriage.

The sex between us was never romantic it was just mechanical and never lasted more than 5 minutes at a time. I guess it was just enough to keep me off his back while all the time he was still sleeping with men. His family and mine had no idea he wasn't the perfect husband who had to put up with a drunken wife.

I remember another incident when he brought home a old class mate to reminisce and have a few drinks and he told me and the kids to go to the Laundromat because he needed some clean clothes. After I got to the Laundromat, I remembered that I'd forgotten the dryer sheets and i started the wash and went back home to get them. When I tried to open the door, the chain lock was on. I called his name for him to open the door, and I heard a lot of shuffling and running. We only had a one bedroom apartment and there was no one in the living area. I looked in the kitchen window and saw my husband coming out of the bedroom pulling up his pants and he opened the door and said he'd forgotten the chain lock was on the door. When I went in the bedroom the guy was lying on the bed with his pants unzipped. My husband claimed they said they were taking a nap but I knew what had happened. i just left and went back to do the laundry and got something to drink again to try to forget about it.

Every time I would ask him if he was gay, he would tell me that I was crazy or drunk and I didn't see what I thought I'd seen. He seemed to become bolder with his affairs, and I knew he was not using protection. One day he dropped me off to go take a GED test and was over two hours late picking me up. When I asked him where he had been, he said the car had broken down. As we walked upstairs to our apartment, I was behind him, and I noticed a big wet spot on the back of his pants. He went in to take a shower and left his pants on the bedroom floor as usual. When I picked them up to see what was on them, I was stunned to see that it was sperm. He had been having sex in the rear and I thought since he was married to me that maybe he liked having sex with guys in their butts, not his, and my heart was broken again. I didn't know what to do. It was so painful.

More things happened, and I learned to look the other way. But I stopped drinking a year ago and started to face my demons. I still see signs of his activities and when I ask him of them he says he's in church now and hasn't had that desire for many years, but my eyes are open now and I see how he looks at other men and I know better. I've started reading a lot of books and joined support groups and now realize it's not going to go away. I'm in college now so that when I leave I can support myself. We sleep in separate rooms and there is no more sex between us. I get checked for the HIV virus every six-months and thank God, so far I'm clean and pray that i stay that way. He does not try to have sex with me anymore and I see it does not even bother him and that tells me what i need to know. I have two grown daughters, and I think they know and are not saying anything to protect their father. They love him so much, and he is a very sweet person to them because although he is gay, he was there for them while I was always drunk. I will not ever forgive myself for that. Maybe someday they will forgive me and understand what I went through and am still going through trying to face this pain sober.

Story 16 – There's Nothing Gay About My Life BY SUZANNE P.

Writing a chapter for a book is a daunting task at the best of times but when the subject matter digs deep into personal relationships and the dreaded SEX word, it then becomes part of the healing process. In fact, I hope it helps others heal with me while I try to understand why I allowed myself to lose who I am and more to the point – why I was content to live without love for 21 years.

My life, the secure sameness I had grown accustomed to, fell apart on Feb 17, 2005 at exactly 2:25pm. I was at work, getting ready for a meeting to discuss my future with the company I worked for, when I received this email from my husband: *"Wanted to give you a heads up that I might be away this weekend, was invited for an over nity at a boy's house! Not my type, kind of feel I should take advantage of the sito – what do you think?"* My response was: "What the HELL!" Then I had to go sit with a committee of 10 executive members and sell myself as the person to become the next CEO of the organization. While the committee was voting, I went back to my computer to find a response from my husband in my email: *"Watch your language! I rec'd an invitation, I was considering it, wanted to involve you, we do have a communication problem but if you'd rather not be involved, so be it. I certainly hope you don't expect me to live the rest of my life as a lie. We will have to discuss this tonight."*

Before going any further, I would like to introduce myself. My name is Suzanne, I am 51 years old and I am also an intelligent, attractive person who strives to be a decent human being. My husband, Doug, is gay and has been since the day I met him. Did I know he was gay? In retrospect yes I did, but as with some women with gay spouses, I denied it to myself and truly believed he loved me, and that we had a great marriage. Doug, like so many gay men, had a full repertoire of reasons why he did not want to make love to me especially in the later part of our marriage. But marriage in my eyes was one of tolerance, support, putting the other person first so I truly tried to understand his reluctance for intimacy. We had all the makings of the perfect couple – both involved in the equestrian world, both competitive, neither wanted children, love of animals, gardening and making a home a place both of you feel good about as well as being a friend through the good and bad. We both grew up in hostile family settings so we were our only family. I was faithful to him in all the years of marriage.

We met thorough the horse world. I was looking for a new horse to purchase and he was working for the barn that was advertising one I was interested in. I ended up purchasing the horse and received a month of free lessons with my future husband.

I was married at the time but the marriage was over and in the process of dissolving. My former spouse was in the music world and I wanted to live in the country, our feelings were not strong enough to compromise. But he was straight and we had a good sex life, so I was not naïve.

The next month was great. I spent almost every day at the farm riding with Doug. He was a great conversationalist, educated, fun and crazy at the same time, as well as sexy and handsome. I was in my element with a country setting with my horses and someone who wanted the same thing as I did. Could life get any better? I moved out to the farm and we began to form our future plans. After six months, we made the first plunge and bought a house with acreage. Doug began to work at the same company as me because we now had a mortgage to pay. We had a circle of friends that went out together as couples or singularly. Those were the days of disco, punk rock and shock value beliefs. We were no different. It was not unusual to go to a punk bar one weekend and then next weekend go to a gay mixed bar. We all wanted to appear so liberal minded and free of all inhibitions. Oddly, drugs were not part of our lifestyle through we did drink like all 20 years old do. Doug was a flirt with both men and women but unapproachable physically. Women always were attracted to him but he was not unfaithful to me with them. He did go out with mutual friends of ours without me, with my blessing, as I was so secure in the fact that he loved me that I could trust him completely. This continued to be my philosophy right up until I received the email last February.

If you are wondering – were we sexually involved right from the beginning? Yes, very much so, from holding hands and kissing in public to regular nighttime sex. We would often get a bottle of wine and share a big cozy chair in front of the fireplace talking for hours on end, with long periods of kissing and exploring. But problems started to crop up about 12 months into the relationship. Doug had been up front about his family life and I knew about his alcoholic, abusive father and enabling mother. I also learned of the darker side of abuse. Doug's father sexually abused him from the age of 13 to 17, forcing him to have oral sex and touch him. His mother knew but did not believe even though his older brother confirmed it. I asked, one day when his father was at our home and drunk, why he did it. I actually received an answer. His father told me about his early teenage years, working with his dad and other men in the mines. There were no women so the young boys were victims of the older men. And it perpetrated a grandfather to father to son lifestyle. Doug actually went to Children's Aid and other agencies to try to talk to counselors but their only contribution was to have his allowance raised. Times were different 25 years ago.

Doug was just short of his 20th year when we met – just three years had passed by since the attacks by his father. He had not healed mentally though we were both too young to understand entirely. And physically he was immature due to lack of intimacy with women. He started to withdraw from me. It was like a second person that despised women that came to replace my friend. He continued to go to work each day and function but he was a robot doing a job. He was paranoid about crowds or people touching him. If we were in a busy store, he would have an anxiety attack and I would lead him to a place of safety. One evening at home, he went somewhere mentally and I found him curled up in a corner of our bedroom acting like a small child. His eyes looked like a deer caught in the headlights when he saw me. He tried to leap out the second story window.

I talked him through this episode with patience and love; in fact he said that when I walked in the room, he saw his Dad instead of me. Then there were the times that he turned on me verbally and said cruel, horrible things. I spoke to our nurse at the office and set up a series of sessions with a male psychologist. He was rude and flirty with the doctor. He would often brag about how easy it was to fool the doctor and mess with his mind. In these sessions, Doug was told that he should leave me and start his own life. Our company nurse would not disclose why but spoke at length to me about leaving Doug as well. He started drinking heavily and went to work for a different company. He was going out bar hopping several times a month with friends and co-workers, most of them I thought I knew.

We began to talk during this time and he opened up to me about his feelings about sex, men and me. He was terrified of being gay and felt that his attraction to men was more of a father figure replacement. He worried that he was the one who encouraged his dad and he was sickened by the thought. He said he was always attracted to older men but sex was not part of the attraction but it was part of the way to get men to notice. He told me about the episodes where he met men as a teenager and went to their homes but always left before sex could be initiated. He had a hard time making friends with men but had many, many women friends from a young age. This was the time period when he said that all he wanted was a wife, home, and security. I was all of those things, plus he was comfortable physically with me. He discussed how he felt that he was asexual, and that he would rather just cuddle.

What woman can resist mothering someone, holding and cuddling with them and feeling secure in the knowledge that only you can help heal a loved one. I was no different. And in time, we both healed. We had gay friends and straight friends then, still do to this day, though the gay friends tend to be women. I was Doug's rock—he had love and affection without pressure as well as an understanding of his father attraction to men. He was still my dashing equestrian mentor and family.

Twenty years flew by. We sold our first home to buy an equestrian center and went into business together in year two. We both loved new and exciting challenges and went on to work outside of our home country. We had our ups and downs like every other couple, but generally had a good life. Our sex life continued to evolve into less and less intercourse until year 10 when it stopped almost altogether. We still slept together, cuddled, and had showers with each other but no actual sex. As we were immersed in each other's lives 24/7, I felt that he was never hugely sexual, and he was just not interested in sex at all.

Was I ever wrong! How could I have shut my eyes to the obvious? That night, after the email last year, we spoke at length. I had to write a prepared speech as words just stuck in my throat. I told him that I still loved him and would continue to be his friend and support his change in lifestyle. It took me almost 30 minutes to say 200 words I was so upset. He sat on the other side of the sofa and acted so calm and superior to my hysterical crying. He told me that he had been seeing men from the very beginning of our relationship, and would I ever be surprised at the men he had been with – lots of our "friends" even the married ones. He said I would be shocked to know of some of the perverted things he had done. What was even more amazing, he honestly thought I knew about all the men and because he was never with a woman, then he was faithful. He felt that his life outside our marriage with his male relationships had absolutely nothing to do with me. I was trying so hard to be the perfect supportive wife, but I was so, so angry at the same time. Twenty-one years wasted without love only to be treated like this. I was financially supporting both of us for the last six years because he wanted to pursue his dream of coaching full time. I did what I always do in moments of high stress; I take all of my emotions and problems, put them in a little box in my mind, and wait until I can deal with them without so much passion.

He did go away that weekend, leaving on the Saturday afternoon to teach a lesson with his overnight bag in hand and then traveling on to his boyfriend's house. I was left totally alone with no one to speak to about this. I started a journal to record my feelings, and I did what almost every woman does in my place. I searched the house for clues; I tried to break into his email and history of sites visited on the Internet. I looked at gay porn and try to visualize him doing this with men. Then I looked for support groups and found Bonnie and her newsletter for wives like me. That was my lifeline to sanity. When he came home Sunday night, I had cleaned myself up (actually I took a good look at myself and did not like what I saw), I made his favorite dinner complete with cherry cheesecake. I was pleasant and cheerful, all the while holding back the tears, asked how his weekend went. He said that he did not really like the guy, and it was an okay weekend. Of course, the angry person in me asked, "Well did you spend the weekend in bed with lots of hot sex?" He was very resentful of that question and told me that it was none of my business, and that it was not what I thought.

Over the ensuing weeks, he spent longer hours out with friends, not our friends but gay men he met through the personals on Yahoo, MSN and the other sites. I read the personals for his and still could not believe it when I would read something like this: *Nice but naughty, bedroom eyes, loves to kiss and cuddle looking for a husband*; complete with a picture of him that he had cut me out of. These creatures of the night he met would call our house and hang up on me when I answered. I changed the machine so it was my voice they heard. I angered one persistent suitor so much that he started leaving messages on the answering machine like – Leroy and I miss you, I just shaved, and Leroy is ready.

My personal journal read like a spiraling plunge into darkness and depression, even though I continued to work and function as if nothing was wrong. I set some basic goals for myself:

1. To be proud of who I am, as a person
2. To be happy with my physical self
3. To learn from my mistakes
4. To meet someone who will love me physically and emotionally as a woman and person, who I can truly trust

My journal itself would fill a book and reading now a year later still brings on an emotional deluge of tears. Some of the comments range from suicidal to loving to anger. Depression was a constant companion. I received the job as CEO and worked long hard hours to cover up the inadequacies in my life. To show how far gone I was – a comment from my journal April 1st, 2005 – "Depression is like cancer, it starts deep down inside without your knowledge or consent. It gradually eats away your self esteem, your confidence, your ability to feel nothing but depression and consumes you till death is the only release."

I spoke to no one about this dark terrible secret. From February to May 2005, Doug went out openly with male friends, one in particular, almost every weekend and a couple of times during the week. As I was at work all day, he was free to do what whatever he wanted. He blamed me for everything wrong in our lives, from financial woes to housekeeping duties. I was able to read his emails without his knowledge and took copies of every one I read. Some of the men he met actually had a decent side to them as they said that he was a nice guy but they won't go out with a married man, as it was not fair to his wife. Doug was in love/lust with the guy he went to stay overnight with, and the emails to this guy were the kind of thoughts and caring I dreamed of, though they never saw each other again as the guy did not feel the same. What was really an eye opener was how he described me to his male friends. One of the more decent quotes from his email: *"I have never loved Suzanne as a wife, she is like a sister to me and she is my family. I do feel guilty each time I leave the house and say goodbye".* He was fond of saying that we were like Will & Grace of the TV sitcom. The one persistent guy, Alex, called three or four times a day. I asked Doug why he did not move out with this guy, and he told me that he really did not like him in that way, and he saw him because he was his only male gay friend.

At this point I am sure everyone would wonder why I did not leave. Between us, we owned 10 horses plus other pets and were leasing a nice property that neither of us would leave. Also my biggest fear was what everyone would say especially as we were so well known in the community. We had many long talks about our future and his life choice, mostly me crying and Doug looking at me like a bug in a jar, with complete bewilderment on his face at my extreme emotions. I gave myself three options on how to deal with him – one was to continue to be a supportive friend and companion, the second was to leave him and pretend that we never knew each other, or the last to scream out to the world about his horrible betrayal and his love of men in order to ruin his reputation and career.

Everything came to a head in May 2005. I decided to be the supportive friend and find my own place. I thought that a chance to be away for the last time together might be a decent ending to our 21-year relationship. So I booked a trip to Mexico to leave on his birthday. I had just turned 50 a few weeks prior and he tried to be nice by saying that I should try to meet someone else, as he was not the husband I wanted him to be. Instead I burst into tears and told him that I have no desire, in fact I was terrified to be with another man. His response–get over it, accept that men are pigs.

The week before our trip was the climax of everything – he had not gone out with any men for a couple of weeks, and I had to leave town for one day. I left early Friday morning and arrived back home in the evening. The house was spotless, grass

STRAIGHT WIVES: SHATTERED LIVES

mowed and Doug was in a great mood. I awoke the next morning and looked over at him and noticed a huge hickey on his neck. I got up quickly and went down to the barn. There I found that our mare had given birth early and the foal was dead. I made it thru the morning only to take my 20 year old cat to the vet and have to him put down. Doug drove me there and all the emotions came spilling out. I was beaten down at last – I was at my worst. We buried the foal and my cat and stood over the grave holding hands, both crying. It was like a symbolic burial of my life, my marriage and my future.

Of course, there was more to this day. I read two emails from Alex to Doug that day – the first one sent earlier in the week saying, *"When are you going to invite me over to visit?. We could do the nasty in the barn or maybe on your bed so I can wipe the man smell all over Suzanne's pillow".* And the second one received that very morning. *"Thanks for having me over to see where you work, play and live. Sorry about our play time, my sunburn did not allow me to get the job done".* So I found out who gave him the hickey. This was the one promise I asked of Doug, that no one comes to our home, as it is my home as well. I said nothing at all to him about what I knew.

That evening we went to bed; I started crying again, very softy so that he would not hear me but he did. He thought it was because of the animals dying so he tried to be comforting to me. A flood gate opened and I tried to tell him how I felt about everything that had happened, that I no longer had a home or family, that I was alienated from my friends, that the house was no longer my home but I did not say a word to him about knowing that Alex was over. He wrote Alex the next day to apologize for not calling but that he was dealing with an emotional wife, perhaps caused by the hickey was his only comments. Again I wrote down my feelings and put them away for a better day. I made it through the week and we went off to Mexico. It was the best vacation we ever had together, no sex but comfortable. Upon our return, Doug wrote to his male friends that he has decided to put his gay life on hold for now and no longer wanted to see them.

It is now almost a year since that time. We are still together with our horses. I recently resigned from my dream job so that I could find something less demanding. I have no visions of my marriage continuing, beyond day to day, even though we are still together and he has not seen anyone since that fateful day last May. He tries to be considerate of my feelings though one nasty comment cut me to the quick last fall – "*I cannot show you any feelings because you will think I care*". We talk about men and his past relationships. What really came across was a bit of a surprise as he talked about actual sex with men. He said that he is a virgin; of course I corrected that as he is not a virgin with me, but he said in the gay world he is virgin because he has never had anal intercourse. He also said that he does not like oral sex but he does enjoy kissing and touching only. He went on to say that is why no man has ever stayed with him nor does he expect any man to want him as a partner. On Valentines Day this year, he put together a thoughtful gift for me with the comment – "I am a great husband except for one thing – Right?"

This life I lead is not a happy one. Any woman contemplating continued marriage with a gay spouse should realize that it will fall apart in time. You will be married to someone who you really will never know or understand and more importantly – trust. Searching for evidence of cheating will become a way of life. You will analyze every conversation to see if there is something hidden in his comments. Every criticism or fault he finds with you will hurt ten times more because you know deep down that he resents the fact that you are a woman. Why do I stay? I am more afraid of the future alone than the loneliness of living with a gay spouse. I am in the process of finding a career totally outside our interests so that I can meet new people and move on one day. Perhaps that is the next chapter in my life.

Story 17: You Deserve a Brighter and Better Tomorrow
by Kristin G.

I have decided to share my story with all of you with the hope that it will help clear some of the confusion surrounding our unique situations. Although I say our situations are unique, I have come to realize there are so many of us out there facing this same situation. A veil of silence exists for many of us in knowing we are straight and find ourselves now married to a gay spouse. While Baby Boomers seem to be affected by this more and more each day, other generations find themselves also faced with this as well. I'd like those who either suspect you may be married to a gay spouse or know you are married to a gay spouse to know you are no longer alone. Your gay spouse may have already come out or worse yet; he still may be in the closet or intends to always stay in the closet and refuses to admit who he really is.

For those who have already come to terms with this situation and the impact it's had on your lives and have chosen the course that's right for you, I applaud and admire you in facing reality and having the courage to take charge of your lives no matter how painful your decisions might be or might have been. For those who continue to struggle and merely exist in your marriages for whatever reasons—like me—I share in your struggle and feel your pain. At times, my life feels like a very shallow and lonely existence. I live on the surface of life and never delve too deep because of the pain and uncertainty associated with this.

None of my closest friends or acquaintances (with the exception of Bonnie's support group) is faced with being married to a gay spouse. After finding out about your gay spouse, some of you have already drawn your own conclusions as to where you stand and what your futures hold. Others may find themselves swirling in a state of immobilization in not knowing where to turn or what lies ahead. This can be very devastating to say the least. Thank goodness for Bonnie's never ending support and the faith that she has for each of us for a brighter and better tomorrow. Those who discover your spouse is gay carry a tremendous burden until you either accept that you are living with a gay spouse or you decide to change your life and no longer tolerate getting less than you deserve in life.

My relationship with my spouse, James, began over five decades ago. We met late in elementary school and had a puppy love relationship that continued in junior high. At the time, James also liked my best girlfriend, and I liked other boys too. What fun times we all had during those carefree innocent years. We enjoyed movies and school dances, as well as playing in band together. James and I liked other girls and boys along the way, but continued our young puppy love relationship through ninth grade. It was at that time, James decided to stop calling. I asked him if there was something wrong and he said everything was fine, but didn't call me or return any of my calls until three years later. When we did finally see one another again, I asked why he stopped calling and his response was "he wanted to see if the grass was greener on the other side of the fence." When I first heard those words, I assumed he meant that he wanted to see what other girls were out there and to sow his oats. I no longer feel certain of the true meaning of those words.

While this should have been a real clue for me to run the other way, I didn't. I think his not being upfront and honest with me at the time was an indication of his immaturity and insensitivity even then. Little did I know it would also be an indicator as to how he would later handle dealing with the realities in his own life, as well as mine. While I fully realized we were both far too young to be in an exclusive relationship and decided to move on, I felt very betrayed and hurt by his not being more honest with me in letting me know what was going on with him at the time. It was like James dropped off the face of the earth and I felt he could care less about my feelings. I questioned how could anyone I trusted and cared about for so long treat me like this? I felt I never wanted to see him again.

Unfortunately, those feelings didn't last forever. I was once again drawn to him three years later after he stopped by my house in my senior year of high school. He had gotten taller, more handsome, and loved his family which I greatly admired. His mother worked, and he was the oldest child at home so he learned to cook, clean, wash clothes, and do yard work. What was even greater, he enjoyed doing all of those household chores. We dated four years before getting married at the age of 21. What a catch he was indeed! We never "went all the way" before getting married, but we did fool around. My parents put the fear of God in me and said if I did anything before getting married, I could get pregnant which would disgrace my family. I wanted to please my parents and do whatever I could to make them happy. Having a baby out of wedlock was not a parent pleaser!

James and I have been married for 38 years and have three children. For the first 10 years of our marriage, our sex life was okay. In retrospect, if I look back, it was pretty boring with little imagination or innovation, but I chalked it up to us not having the experience others had had and in time. However, I was optimistic and knew it would certainly get better. We lived in a different era and didn't have all the sexual exposure and toys that one has at their disposal today. Experimenting sexually was totally foreign to both of us so I accepted our sexual relationship as just being naïve in not wanting to go "out of the box" in trying new and more exciting approaches to a more fulfilling sexual life.

After 10 years of marriage, I discovered that my husband became interested in a mutual friend and one of his office co-workers. Although I cannot prove their involvement, I heard later that they took extra long lunches and it was obvious to others they cared for each other in more than an office friendship way. I confronted my husband and he said he was flattered because she paid more attention to him than me. He professed to love only me and wanted us to be together throughout eternity. By the way, I was pregnant at the time with our second child. Once again, I should have grabbed a clue, but was committed to doing whatever it took to fix me so I could become the wife he truly wanted to be with. In hindsight, maybe he was trying to prove something more to himself by being attracted to another female rather than a male.

Our lives together have been primarily wrapped around our children, their lives, and their activities. After being married for 10 years, we began having silly arguments all the time for no apparent reason. Once again, I decided to do what I could and sought professional counseling to save our marriage. I also felt that whenever you go to marriage counseling, sooner or later the counselor typically wants to also include the spouse. I didn't know if my James would go to counseling or not, but I felt that if he refused, that would tell me he really wasn't interested in saving our marriage. I could then go on with my life knowing I had done all I could to hold our marriage together.

I selected this particular counselor because he was a Christian, and I felt he wouldn't recommend me getting a divorce without serious consideration. At that time, I hated the idea of being a divorce statistic and the stigma surrounding a divorce, but if it meant that, I was prepared to wear the scarlet letter "D" for the remainder of my life. I had to also deal with what would God think of me possibly breaking my marriage vows, and would I end up in heaven or not when I died?

Aside from this, we also had two children and my parents who thought the world of James. Earlier in our marriage, he had always been good about doing the right thing and was a great host whenever my parents were around. By the way, the counselor's assessment was that James and I were not good communicators and we needed to work on this in order to have a successful marriage. Little did I know at the time what the real core issue was deteriorating our marriage.

There were signs ten years after being married or possibly even before that our marriage was different than our closest friends who were married. By that, I mean we did not dress or undress in front of one another; we didn't share financial matters, nor did James communicate with the same level of respect towards me around our friends and family. He has been verbally abusive during the majority of our marriage. I was very naive to think that James really took care of me by paying our bills and keeping me totally out of the loop. I now realize and see this as a real control issue and an all out effort to keep me in the dark. He would include me in our finances only when we needed to take out a loan for something if he needed my signature.

One day, James told me not to go into the trunk of our car as he had a present for me that he didn't want me to see. Although I tried to honor his request, my gut instinct told me something was different in the way he was acting. I found out that "my present" was actually a pair of men's provocative underwear. I first thought I might be seeing this underwear, and it excited me that we might be in for some fun surprises. Little did I know that I never did see "my present" ever again and my surprises continued throughout FOUR decades!

"My discoveries" included male porn videos, more provocative underwear, lubricants, condoms, leather items, various subscriptions to gay magazines, and a secret post office box. After seeing these items, I became immobilized and didn't know where to turn. I no longer suspected my husband was gay, <u>I knew he was gay</u> although he did not know I knew.

It took me three years to weigh how to approach my husband about being homosexual—three years! During these three years, I feel that I went through the Stages of Grief that Kubler-Ross identifies as: Denial, Anger, Bargaining, Depression, and Acceptance. While I feel the first four are self-explanatory, I feel what Acceptance means to me is admitting to myself that my husband was/is and will always be a gay man and to then realize that I could never fix something that was truly never mine to fix no matter what. These five Stages of Grief each came with their own share of heartache, pain, loneliness, and tears. Our sex life had become non-existent for several years.

Throughout our marriage, I was always trying to find a way to better myself and try and find the answer to what was wrong with ME. I question really if James was ever truly "mine" from the very beginning of our marriage. Once again, I feel I will never know the real truth. At times, I was critical of James, but never seemed to realize that he could use some serious fixing, too. I kept trying to do what I needed to do to make things better. I am a peacemaker…not a heartbreaker.

I had gained weight and I was buying self-help books on topics that I felt might help a hopeless situation. My ship was sinking and there was nothing I could do to stop it. Basically, even though I knew my husband was gay and in the closet, I still felt it was my fault for marrying him and not reading the earlier signs in our relationship. I felt responsible and therefore, it was up to me to turn this around and create a more positive environment for us to live in while figuring it out. As time went on, I knew this was no longer possible to continue this charade. I was devastated after fully admitting and realizing our marriage was in shambles (even though it had been for many years). I became part of Bonnie's growing support group members after hearing Bonnie on a local television station five years ago. For once, the things I heard Bonnie say in this interview made sense and were all things that were going on in my own life.

I want to say that I am not a victim. It is no one else's fault that my husband is gay, and that I am currently in a gay/straight marriage. I did not know my husband was gay when we married. Perhaps he didn't know or fully know or want to admit what his true sexual orientation was at the time. This I'll never know as I feel my husband refuses to acknowledge who he really is and therefore lies or denies any truths associated with his being gay. I have chosen to stay in my marriage for the number of years I have for the sake of our children, family, family holidays (graduations, weddings, births, etc., etc.) and now for our grandchildren. In addition to those reasons listed above, there have been far more excuses than I ever care to admit. Earlier in my marriage, I felt staying in my marriage provided me with the financial security I needed to survive the lifestyle I was accustomed to living, when in reality; it provides me with a very false sense of security. I have a plan for my future, but am hesitant to say where it will lead me.

Our children are grown and we now have grandchildren. James is so loving and affectionate towards our children and grandchildren, but that's as far as it goes. He remains very much in the closet about being gay. He does not want to discuss it with anyone including his children or me. Everything is on his terms. It is obvious that we both exist in a loveless marriage, but neither of us has yet to "pull the plug." James said he'd had hoped he could take being gay to his grave. Because of my confronting him about being gay, the best he could do to acknowledge he is gay was to say, "You're probably right."

Because none of our friends know James is gay, they keep telling me how lucky I am that our kids are grown and we are able to travel to such wonderful places. By remaining silent, I also feel I'm in the closet along with James and have compromised who I truly am and who I want to be. It is getting more difficult to live under these circumstances. Life is passing me by and I am not being true to myself in living the life I deserve. This is what hurts the most. James is very controlling and secretive. For example, he gets and opens all our mail and doesn't share it unless it has my name on it; takes care of our bills (or does he?), bleaches his teeth and goes tanning and denies doing either, picks out and buys all our furniture, bedding, and all other household accessories; belongs to Net Flicks and selects all our movies because he alone maintains our password and won't share it with me. He says if I can pay for them, then I can pick them out. He continues to have a secret post office box, buy gay porn videos, subscribe to gay magazines, purchase items from his magazines, and I'm sure other things that I'll never know about. Why oh why do I stay??

I feel I have paid a tremendous price and have given up the better part of my life with someone who only cares about himself in order to maintain his secret life. If any gay person is out there reading this, know you are not sparing us from being hurt by not being honest in admitting you're gay. Although the truth will hurt, the lies and deceit will hurt more and will cause far greater pain than you'll ever imagine possible. I have come home from work on several occasions and found James in a compromising position "satisfying" his needs. This makes me sick and makes me feel like we both need to get on with our lives. Sadly, he won't be the one making that call and feel it will be up to me to "break the family apart" as my mother puts it. I want to have a home where I feel safe after being at work all day and a place where I can relax, have my tastes represented, and feel good about myself. As of today, this is truly not the case. I know that James is dealing with his own issues, but I can no longer be responsible for him refusing to accept his true self and live his life accordingly.

For those reading this book, I'd like you to think about what's going on in your life. Do your marriage and your relationship make sense and is it right for you? Are you sacrificing who you are or where you want to be? Most of us in Bonnie's group did not plan on facing this in our lives nor did we save money for a divorce, but each of us has a right to our own happiness. If someone has taken that away from you, it's time to get it back. Rely on your better instincts to help guide you and be brutally honest with yourself in admitting what's really going on in your lives.

Time passes much too quickly. We all need to realize that none of us are guaranteed a tomorrow, but we can do our best to make today a better day. If you see a part of me in you, please don't wait as long as I have to figure your lives out. I have put everyone else before me and in retrospect, I feel that was wrong. If you take care of yourself first, then you will be better prepared to handle everything else that comes along in life. Marriage does not nor should it be this difficult or one sided. True love means open communication, respect, compromise, honesty, integrity, and sexual fulfillment. It should not be based on lies and deceit. Life is far too precious to not live in peace and harmony. Even the most difficult situations can be conquered with the strength that is in each and every one of us. Although I have not worked all the details out in my life, I am working towards my discovering who I really am and finding my "true peace" in this world. I remain committed and dedicated to this effort and I'll never give up hope for a brighter and better tomorrow.

Bonnie is and has been my true inspiration. She continues to have faith in me and has never gives up on me. I am eternally grateful for her true devotion, loyal support, guidance, and most of all, her loving and never ending friendship.

Story 18: Left Him By Nina A.

This was the title of a story I read sitting in train four years ago, when my husband forcefully took me to India. Within two days of our arrival in New Delhi, he took me to the station with seven peaces of luggage and said a final goodbye as he put me on train to go to the city where I lived before marriage. I had a side seat in the train, which is very small and good for me to give me time to think alone. I drew the curtains, got my private little area, where, no one could see me crying.

As I was reading the story, I was weeping like a child. I felt so relieved, to know I am not the only one going through the nightmare. I never wish anyone to have any suffering ever, but at that moment, that story worked like a pain killer. I was not sure if, it was a real story or a friction. I got so much encouragement from that story, I thought in my mind, I will not let him make me crazy for saving face for him. I will make myself strong and go back To USA, and will not let this happen to me.

The reason it is important to me, to write my story is that—just like I got inspired by the story, someone else may get strength and courage to get out of the situation and not be afraid because the unknown is scary. I know how smart women are, in India also, and lot has been changed since I first left India. All my friends are making sure, that their daughters are not only educated but also working and living the life they deserve. This message is more for, everyone, who is stuck and thinks life is over. Life is not a dress rehearsal; you get only one chance so live it.

When I came to the USA, I was very young, married and a mother of a three months old baby boy, not knowing anything at all. I was very innocent and had not even developed my identity. In my culture, you are told not to have strong opinions about anything otherwise you will have lots of problems when you get married and go to your n-law's home. Actually, that was one of the reason parents used to get their daughters married very young, so they could be molded easily in new surroundings. But the truth is change is certain and sooner or later everyone struggles and wants to know "who I am."

Our culture is very rich and families are very closely knit, and everyone has obligations towards other people to the extent that you can't live your own life and suffocate, or if you have courage to speak, then maybe you change your life. But the unknown is scary so everyone just keeps on suffering and life goes on. Living in a society where you are always worried about "what others will think" you always has to live two faced life.

As I am writing, I am realizing for the first time I have changed being in America. I became an American woman, who now at fifty is asking for her rights and is not compromising her dignity because I grew, and I am aware of the world around me. That's why I am able to raise my voice. Even being in America, it would not have been possible for me if my both of my children wouldn't have supported me. I know many of my friends, who are suffering for different reasons, find themselves stuck. The reason of all the suffering is our culture and traditions means more then anything else. We all came to this country a long time ago and became very American on surface, but we were living in a totally Indian way with our culture Our children are American although they grew up in Indian Home. They got best of both worlds, and I am so happy for them.

Because of our culture and being the eldest in the family, no one ever imagined that my husband was living a secret life. He was known for his charming personality, and he was always very quiet and calm. I didn't know there are people who are gay. If I did, I would have known forever of his being gay. Now looking back, I know why he was different, and why I was always frustrated. I can even recall something he said to me when we were newly wed which had made no sense at the time. He said that one of my brothers-in-law had told me being a guy you are not supposed to approach the partner in the bed, and I totally believed that. In the 1950's, girls used to be very naive in India, especially in the small towns.

We were very different people...I am very fun loving happy go lucky type. I love to do things instantly like enjoy going out, watching movies, listening to the music, and meeting people. He was not interested in any of it. I always had to force him to do anything. If I needed company, I would talk with him, and he will listen; he was a great listener. He didn't tell me even a single story from his childhood, but I would not stop telling mine.

I always craved affection and missed hugs and kisses and was giving him so much but he never reciprocated. I kept wondering what's wrong with me that he is not attracted to me. To make it worse, he always had something bad to say about my body.

People enjoy my company, and I was always invited in gatherings, because of my funny nature. I am very passionate person, so there was no lack of affection from my side. He criticized me for everything I did and made me feel so bad all the time. My self steam was very low. I used to tell him all the time that you are chipping away my heart slowly, very slowly.

He would stand in front of the mirror after the shower and look at himself but nothing ever crossed my mind. I used to keep my emotions shut down by eating and always chewing boatel nuts. He complained of my chewing all the time and made fun of me. Only now I realized that was also to suppress my feelings. Ever since he left, I am not chewing constantly.

The year 2000 turned out to be bad for us. Who knew it was the beginning of his planning to live his authentic self. He used to joke with me about having sex with someone else, and why I have a problem. He had started talking about people going through divorce after kids are gone. I remember saying in response that I can understand—you can't keep living in misery forever. I didn't know he was talking about himself.

I saw him filling out personal sites and asked him why. He very conveniently said for Sam its only $19 for three months. I asked why on this site? Maybe Sam wants to marry an Indian girl plus why would you be looking for him? I can't believe I didn't get suspicious even then.

He would come home, eat dinner and start talking to this man for couple of hours. It was work related and I would be bored but tell people he is a workaholic. If he was not talking on phone, then we would sit in front of sofa and he have his computer on his lap and sit near me, while I watched TV passing my time. We were having lot of problems in the relationship because of our extended family. We also had our own issues. There is lot of pressure on males to take care of their family. We came to USA so young and have changed with time and didn't have all the facilities servants, cooks and maid. So I waited for the day when my own kids went to collage so I can be free and do all the things I have always wanted to do. Just then his sister with her whole family came to USA with a green card and wanted us to keep her boys while she returned to India to work until she retired. That was the biggest reason for a huge conflict between us. While her son stayed at our place for six months, we were having fights almost on a daily basis. The same man, who never enjoyed movies with me would sit with his nephew for three hours and enjoy the movie. Life was hell.

Then came the invitation for my sister's son's wedding. No one from my family wanted me to go because my husband didn't have a job and the wedding was in India. But he kept telling me not to worry and I must go, and "you will thank me later for sending you." When I said I would go for 2 weeks, he insisted that I go for as long as I wish because going to India is not that easy. He got me a ticket for five weeks.

How can I forget my arrival home? All had changed. The minute i saw him, I knew something was not right. I asked him what is wrong and why he looked so different and pale. He said it was because he missed me. I was happy to hear that, and it made sense, but a few minutes later he started fighting about my heavy luggage, and we were fighting in the car. I was mad thinking here I am dying to see him, and he was getting angry.

From that moment on, it never got better. I was feeling something was very wrong, like I was living with a totally different person. He would not bathe until midday, no shaving for days, and would not move from the computer for hours at a time. I was looking very hard and asking him questions. Why was I he ignoring me and what is going on? My husband, who is quite ingenious, kept his calm and asked me to go to see the OBGYN, as I may be going through menopause causing me to be depressed.

My sister called from India after my return and he wanted to talk to her. He asked her if someone raped me when we were traveling in India. He told her, "Your sister is going crazy, and not listening to me. Why don't you ask her to seek help?" My sister was so shocked and didn't know what he was talking about. She told him that she was with me for five weeks and I was just fine. Both the kids weren't home, so he had nothing to worry about, and whenever they came he was behaving so normal, that no matter what I was saying, they didn't listen to me. I was complaining about him, but he was not saying anything, so the kids were not able to see any change in him. They also started thinking "dad is right—mom is having some problem." I was so alone because no one was listening to me. He started telling everyone that I am going crazy, and am not seeking help. I was so helpless and mad at everyone for not understanding me.

One night, I woke up crying as I often did in the middle of the night and asked him what is going on. Then I saw a young guy in my back yard. I came back in the bedroom and told him. He said I went insane. The next morning I said, "Tell me all the truth. I want to meet the person." He said, "Oh my God, now you started seeing people too." He said very calmly, "Honey please, lets go to the doctor. I will also go and get help," as if I was crazy. In response, I would scream so he could use that against me. He was pushing all the right buttons, and I was not realizing his game. He made such a sad faces and showed everyone how sorry he is that his wife became mentally ill.

The next day I told my brother who lives in Montreal about the man in the yard and he told me to come over right away. I cried my heart out and asked for help. I was very anxious, so my sister-in-law suggested I take a pill to relax and do lot of yoga and take care of myself. I will never forget that. My brother didn't do anything and my husband told him that I was crying all the time and was anxious. Without questioning, everyone assumed I was disturbed and my husband was right.

Once I got back from Montreal, my husband realized that he was able to fool everyone. He started taking me everywhere with him and asked me if I am still seeing anyone. I was so angry at him that he had to prove me crazy to save face. I was lost and was looking for help.

He came up with this condition called schizophrenia and told the therapist about it and asked her to send me to a psychiatrist. His only purpose to take me to psychiatrist was to get me medicine so he could tell everyone I was crazy.

Every time I caught him, he would say I am seeing people, and he kept doing that for whole year until I realized his game. I never had to hide anything plus you can totally tell from my face whether I am angry or happy. I can't hide my emotions while he is expert in that field. My kids think their Dad is a boring and quiet and contained man; they have no idea of his other side. He was unhappy because he was living with a wrong person— namely a straight wife, and seeing me so happy and singing and having fun talking with friends and the kids. This was making him angrier.

He thought I was not missing anything because he is the one who is suffering. Here I am, a very sad woman, thinking it was my destiny and was making the best of the situation, never knowing what real relationship is or how a man treats a woman. When my son opens a door for me, I always felt odd, and tell him that I wonder who will be the lucky woman to get this treatment, not realizing how very normal it was for man to do for a woman.

I have family full of doctors; one of my brothers is even a psychiatrist. When he called to say hello, my husband went out of his way to tell him that I am accusing him of surfing porno sites. Until that day I didn't know what porno sites were. My brother suggested medicine to calm me down, and my husband used against me saying, "Even your brother thinks you are depressed and need help."

I was struggling not to fall apart. I was seeking whatever help was available and did whatever I needed to be healthy and not become sick. I started dhan yoga and read lots of self help books. I tried to write to several American men on the Internet seeking support and friendship. One particular person came to help and vanished like a spirit, but he guided me through my whole ordeal. Here my husband and kids were taking me to therapist, while my husband was working hard to prove me mentally ill, and there I was asking this person what I should do next. My husband kept wondering how I was getting this strong, and not knowing, he kept accusing my sister and other family members of destroying the family and not letting me seek medical help.

Thanks to this person (to me it was a spirit) wherever he is. I was begging my kids to listen to me, but they also insisted that I should go for therapy. They couldn't and will never be able to tell because no one can read my spouse. He is so good at it. But GOD IS GREAT, nothing lasts forever—at least that's my hope.

Within these past four years, I went away several times, and then he started traveling for business. We weren't together much, and every time he came back it was the same old story. "You are mental and need treatment." I was so sick of his games, lying and keeping an innocent face. At the same time I was getting stronger and living happily because of my son took care of my financial needs and always said, "Mamma (that's what he calls me) I love you and I will always take care of you."

My daughter gave me backbone while I was falling apart. She kept me with her while studying law, rented an apartment and said, "Mom, I am living with you, so don't think even for once that you are dependent on me; it's your household, and I am living with my mom." I would have never made it without these two who love their father equally and have never questioned him. ARE THEY ANGELS OR WHAT?

Today is my birthday and my daughter is graduating. My husband who has been in India also came and my son is also here. This will be the last time all four of us are together, as far as I am concerned, except when kids get married. Because of our culture, there is no discussion of separation, divorce, or money matters. Both of us want to make some final decision, but there is no one who can make it happen as in the last four years he made sure I am not in touch with any of his family members because he convinced them that I am mentally ill. My family is trying to stick beside me, although we did have arguments and I am mad at them for not being there for me. My kids know it's over but wish they could fix it. My struggle is not over, but the flip side is I am very strong and living with dignity, and will not compromise my new found self-esteem and love for myself.

Today is 26th of May 2006. My daughter graduated from BC Law.

Now that we are done with Boston, we are moving to San Francisco where my son is already working and my daughter also has a job waiting there. So this is the end of chapter one.

I will be in touch with Bonnie our Lifesaver. What a great purpose she found in her life. I am hoping to do the same for women in India some day.

Love you all.

Story 19 - Love and Deception By Camille B.

I met the man who was to become my husband a few days before my twentieth birthday at the apartment of a mutual friend. I was a sophomore in college while he was twenty-three years old and in the second year of graduate school finishing work on a Master's Degree. For me it was love at first sight, but not for him. I spent an hour or so with him and my friend that evening, and then I didn't see him again until the fall of that same year when I moved in with my friend to share an apartment. My future husband and his roommate managed the small apartment building. We saw each other frequently. His roommate, my friend, and I would get together to play games, play cards and have dinners together, but he never asked me out. I knew he was a serious student and was working hard at his studies, but I kept hoping he would ask me out. I dated other boys in my classes who asked me out, but I really only wanted to go out with the one person who didn't ask me.

That year he did finish his Master's Degree, applied for and was accepted into a doctoral program in another state. In the late summer he moved away and I thought I would never get a chance to go out with him. When he moved away though, we began writing letters to each other on a very regular basis and it was through these letters that we became closer and declared our love for each other.

I was now in my senior year of college. When he came home for Christmas break he introduced me to his family. Before he returned to school we made plans for me to come visit him during the summer after I finished my senior year of college, which I did. I drove out to where he was attending graduate school and spent the summer living with him.

During this time we did have our first sex together. He was a virgin, I was not. He needed help the first time because he didn't know what to do. Our sex life got better as the summer went on, and it seemed okay to me. I previously had sex before with men, but only three times, so I was not very experienced myself. He never tried to kiss me except during sex. He didn't hug me or show any kind of the playful sexual behavior I saw among our friends who were couples. I think I was so in love with him that that was the reason I didn't question myself as to why his behavior was so different from previous boyfriends whose main goal seemed to get me into bed, the sooner the better, or different from the behavior I saw among our friends who were couples. Their behavior was playful and affectionate; our relationship was never like that.

When summer was over and it was time for me to return home, I didn't want to go. and he said he didn't want me to go either. We became engaged. We set a wedding date during his Christmas break in January. I returned home to plan the wedding, and we got married as planned.

I worked full time while he finished his doctorate. I had changed my major during the beginning of my junior year and therefore needed a few more credits to finish my degree. Our plan was that I would work until he finished his doctorate and then when he had a job, I would return to college and finish my degree and then on the graduate school.

To me our sex life seemed normal and I had no complaints at that time. By now we had been married not quite three years. He graduated and got a job in the University town we now live in. I immediately applied for admission to the University and was accepted, but I did not start attending classes in the fall as I had planned. He wanted to buy a house first and wanted me to keep working for awhile, so I did. This was just the beginning of many attempts by me to return to school to finish my degree. Unhappily I never did finish, he always managed to put up one roadblock after another throughout our marriage. It was never convenient to him for me to return to school.

After being married for three years, we were ready to start a family, but we both had infertility problems. We tried all the treatments available at the time, but we still were not successful in becoming pregnant. We took some time to decide whether or not we would adopt children or remain childless. He had helped raise his younger brother and two sisters, so he said he would go along with whatever I decided. I wanted to be a mother, and so we decided we would have a family through adoption.

We adopted two children, first a boy and then a girl. We were very happy. He worked and I stayed home with the children. By the time we adopted our son, we had been married eight years and our daughter arrived not long after our tenth anniversary. I was sure we would be the oldest parents in their kindergarten classes, but of course we weren't!

Our children were both adopted from the same foreign country. Our son arrived seemingly healthy, but it turned out that he has a serious mental illness, and we have had a lot of problems raising him, causing friction between my husband and me. Our daughter arrived with a birth defect which we had corrected with neurosurgery when she was five months old. Twelve years later we found out she had been given a transfusion during that surgery that contained the Hepatitis C virus and she was infected. She went through a clinical trial at our local Children's Hospital for eleven months that was successful and now after five years is considered cured. My daughter is now healthy and in college and my son seems to be trying to get his life back on the right track. We had had a lot on our plate for many years with our children and that may be why I did not initially notice some of the signs that my husband was gay.

When our son was ten, we had been married for nearly eighteen years. My husband went to the video store with our son and rented two gay porn videos while my son rented a Nintendo game. I later found out that my son saw what his father rented and guessed from that time on his dad was gay or suspected his dad was gay. My son has never told his father what he saw him rent that day.

My husband brought these videos home and showed them to me that evening. I asked him why he had rented gay porn, he acted surprised. He said he must have picked it by accident because he meant to rent regular porn. My reply was one video maybe, but two? He asked me if I wanted to watch them, and he said he was curious. I said no, I was not curious and went to bed. He stayed up and watched them both. He accidentally rented gay porn again the next time he went to the video store, and this time I confronted him and asked him he was gay? He denied it, of course, I was not going to let the subject drop so, I brought up two male friends he had in the past. One man was openly gay and he saw a lot of him and sometimes the three of us went out to dinner together. The other man he introduced me to I was sure was gay as soon as I met him, but my husband told me I was crazy. He said this man had been married, was divorced, and had custody of his two children and was raising them himself. I suppose at the time I was quieted by the fact that this man had been married, thinking that if he had been married surely he couldn't be gay, right? I pointed out to my husband that at one time he and the second man had practically been inseparable and then this man seemed to literally fall off the face of the earth. All of a sudden I only heard negative things about this man where once I had only heard my husband sing his praises. Now I believe they probably had had an affair, but this is 20/20 hindsight. At the time I was either in denial or oblivious, I am not sure which.

For all the years we had been married, this is what I knew to be a normal sex life for us. Before we could have sex, first my husband had to smoke marijuana or snort some cocaine and/or drink alcohol. We both had to take showers before sex, but never together. I suggested we shower together once early on in our marriage he was against it from the beginning. He just did not like the idea of it. We only had sex in the bedroom and only in the bed. The room had to be pitch dark. My attempts to light candles to make the room romantic were met with disapproval and the candles were blown out right away. He wanted no light in the room. We had to be under the covers. He liked to have me perform oral sex on him, and he was happy to perform oral sex on me too, but when it came to intercourse, he would often lose his erection.

This became increasingly frustrating for me. I told him that I wanted the intercourse because it made me feel close to him, but the only position he could keep an erection in was from behind, which did not give me the closeness I needed. This was his preferred position for intercourse. His preference was really that I just perform oral sex on him until he reached orgasm and then he would do the same for me. He was not selfish in that he did care that I also had an orgasm, but it was not in the way I wanted to achieve it, but the way he wanted me to achieve it.

It was later that I realized that my husband had to be on drugs and/or alcohol, not be able to see me, I had to be squeaky clean and covered up before he could face having sex with me, and then his preferred position was not face to face, but from behind where he didn't have to look at me. Once I realized this, not only were my feelings hurt, but I also wanted to talk to him about it. As I would learn, this was only one of many issues he was unwilling to discuss with me.

After he brought home the gay porn, the next thing to happen was that I caught him numerous times on the computer looking at gay porn and masturbating in the evening. One time though during the day, my daughter and I came home to find him in the study looking at gay porn on the computer, masturbating with the curtains open. It was lucky that I was walking ahead of my daughter. She was about seventeen at the time and could say something to him before she stepped into sight. It was a work day and he should have been at work. I guess it was to be a lunchtime quickie, and he thought my daughter and I would be out of the house longer than we were. I was furious…it was such a close call. What if our daughter had been in front of me and seen her dad first?

I would have thought this should have put some fear into him, but this kind of behavior continued right up until our divorce; in fact it got worse. He seemed to be willing to take so many risks, more and more as time went on. Our sex life tapered off during the last eight or nine years of our marriage until we were having sex once a month, once every three to four months and then one day it just stopped without any explanation. I asked him why, but he didn't answer me. This became very common, he wouldn't answer my questions, just stare at me.

The last six years of our marriage we did not have any sex, and it wasn't until the last few months of our marriage that he was willing to discuss anything with me. When I would ask him for sex, at first he made excuses, like he was tired or had a headache, then he simply said no and that was that. He made me feel like it was my fault, yet wouldn't tell me what I had done wrong. Blaming me for our problems and not explaining what I had done wrong became a pattern. I was feeling very guilty, but I didn't know how to fix the problems because he wouldn't discuss with me what I had done to cause all our problems. He just would say that they were my fault. I took on the blame and he was happy to let me.

There is another incident that I still do not know the truth about. The last year we were married I found a pink "While You Were Out" slip in my car. It was the kind of message pad you use when someone is out of the office. My husband had borrowed my car, and the next time I was in it I happened to see this pink piece of paper crumpled in the cup holder. I opened it up and it had the following written on it: "5"7" Latino". I took the paper into the house and asked my husband about it. He got a very surprised look on his face, grabbed the paper out of my hand, and threw it into the garbage. He almost took my hand off in the process. I told him I already read it and what did it mean? He was furious, but offered no explanation. Over time I was told at least three different explanations about what that piece of paper meant. He offered different explanations in our therapist's office during marriage counseling. None of the explanations included him meeting a man for sex, which is what I believe. One was he was buying me a stolen jade statue for my birthday, that was so absurd I had to laugh, he was buying drugs, and the last he wasn't doing anything and the paper didn't mean anything.

Here are some other incidents that happened during the end of the marriage. He would meet his friends, always men I had never heard of or met for dinner, but only in the large city we live near that has a large gay community. He started smoking crack cocaine, snorting cocaine and smoking methamphetamine on a regular basis. He would be up for days at a time and then crash. His longtime friends at work were noticing a change in his behavior and calling me asking questions. They guessed that he was coming to work high. They told me that he would leave work during the day for hours and then come back in the early afternoon or not at all. He never let on to me that he was leaving work as I was being told, and I did not tell him that I knew about this.

He was angry much of the time with me and our daughter over nothing. He had often been angry with me, but never with our daughter, but now he was treating her differently, and she was upset much of the time. I found a glass pipe and a few rocks of methamphetamine in our basement bathroom along with a glass pipe when I went down to iron a shirt one morning. I was upset because again I was concerned about what explanation he would offer our daughter if she had found it instead of me. It was lying out on the counter in plain sight. I was very upset and had words with my husband about this. I told him if he left drugs around and our daughter found them, he would have to explain to her what they were doing there. At this point our son was no longer living at home, so we only had our daughter at home.

One afternoon the three of us did all come home together. We had all been to our daughter's college orientation is a city about an hour from our home. Our daughter had stayed in the dorm overnight, and I in a hotel. My husband was supposed to stay with me, but drove home and did not return until the next morning at 6:00 a.m. looking like he hadn't slept and disheveled. When the three of us returned home in the afternoon and walked into the house, our daughter walked into the family room and found a glass pipe on the family room floor and picked it up. She knew what it was from drug education classes in high school. She turned, looked at me, and then at her father. He, of course, was immediately mad at me. He grabbed the pipe from her, and she ran off to her room and told him he had some explaining to do, first to me and then to her.

We did not want to tell our daughter that her father had been smoking methamphetamines, so I agreed to let him tell her that he had been smoking marijuana. At her age and with the information they get in school about drugs, she may have known it wasn't from marijuana because it didn't smell like it. I don't know. That was about the last straw. I knew that as soon as our daughter graduated from high school I was going to file for divorce, but I wanted to hear him say he was gay. There were so many incidents that made me suspicious and when I would confront him about them he would offer no excuse or make me feel as if I was crazy or imagining things. It was so frustrating. There were so many days that I fought depression and even contemplated suicide because there was such disorder in my life. I've learned from the other women who are part of our support chats that the feeling of hopelessness is so common where there seems to be no hope.

I went online and typed in straight wives + gay husbands and Bonnie Kaye's website came up. I read everything on it. I went right out and bought her book and read it, and then I emailed Bonnie for help. Like many women, I told Bonnie I wanted a confession and Bonnie told me as she has told many others.

"Don't wait for a confession". I did give my husband Bonnie's book to read anyway and he did read it much to my surprise. He came out of the bedroom and said, "I am gay". I heard the words I needed to hear. I told him I wanted a divorce and filed the next day.

Being married to a gay man robs you of your self-esteem and your life. In my case my husband made it so difficult for me to return to college, I never did finish my college degree in the almost thirty years we were married. He didn't want me to work, so I didn't. He always found ways to keep me from going back to work or making it impossible for me to keep working if I found a job and was hired. I was completely dependent on him for everything and that is how he controlled me. I am a fifty-three year old woman who had been out of the job market for twenty-three years. I have no real marketable skills, but I have to go back to work when most people are thinking towards retirement. The jobs I can get hired for are not very challenging for me, but the type of job that I would find interesting and challenging I don't have the credentials for. My ex-husband is bitter about the divorce settlement even though we followed the divorce laws of our state and complains about it to everyone including our children. He is mad at me for divorcing him. He proposed we stay married and each of us date, that way we could keep "his" money together. I told him no. He tells anyone who will listen what a horrible person "I" am, but I haven't done anything, he is the one who lied not me.

He maintained he had never been unfaithful to me and in the next breath suggested I get tested for HIV, which I did the next day. He was cruel in many ways towards me, especially verbally abusive. He could not talk to me in a civil tone or without screaming at me for almost a year, he still has trouble talking to me with out being insulting or blaming me for something.

He told me he knew was gay on our wedding day, but if he had told me the truth I would have called off the wedding. He is right—I would have. He cannot understand why I feel used. He feels since he provided a nice home, food and nice lifestyle for the children and me, he hasn't done anything wrong. He met our basic needs in his mind, but really he didn't. He lied about who he really is. Our marriage was based on a lie, but he does not agree with that. He seems unable to take any responsibility for his actions and the pain it has caused me, our children and our families. He has known from the beginning that for me it was love at first sight. I remember asking him throughout our marriage when he first realized he was in love with me before we got married, I am still waiting for an answer to that question. I do not believe he ever was in love with me, perhaps he did love me to the best of his ability to love a woman, I don't know.

Life does go on though. I have begun a new life and new home to go with it. I am living alone for the first time in my life, and I love it. I have dated some and had a relationship with a straight man that showed me how wonderful sex can be. There is nothing wrong with me as my husband had me believe. That relationship did wonders for my self-esteem. It affirmed to me that I am desirable, sexy, and attractive. My partner was sexually playful, he couldn't keep his hands off me and I loved it. It was wonderful and just what I needed to feel like a woman again.

I would like to end with a message of hope to anyone reading this. I know how sad and hopeless you feel because I have been there and felt the same way. You just cannot image your life ever being anything but what it is right now. Getting through each and every day takes all the energy you have and then some. It can be better, but you have to take the first baby steps to get out of your situation. It won't happen overnight, but little by little your life can get better. Find a friend or someone you feel safe confiding in so you don't have to carry this burden alone. Make a plan to get out. It may take time and may not be easy, but take that first step. I no longer let my husband treat me with disrespect without at least standing up for myself, because I was told that people treat you like you let them.

If you have suspicions that your husband is gay, go with your gut feelings because you are probably right. He will keep the truth from you at all costs and do not wait for a confession because according to Bonnie Kaye, chances are you will never get it. There are many women out here just like you, and we understand what you are going through and are here to help— we just need to know how to contact you.

Story 20 - The Ball Cards Came Out of the Closet Too
– Jennifer E.

Midwestern summers are usually hot and muggy; however, the summer of 1984 was surprisingly comfortable. August is normally the height of heat in Kansas City, but we didn't have any major heat wave with temperatures soaring into the century mark that year. I was 27 years old had just started a new job at a locally owned bank and was in the process of purchasing my first home. I was a single woman with a college degree, had all the confidence in the world and a future full of hope. I met Joe.

Joe also worked at the bank; he was in audit while I was in retail investments. The courtship began in a very friendly way. We got along well, like having a best friend. I was actually dating another man, a six-foot four lawyer, blond with blue eyes, very much like all the other men I had ever taken an interest in. But then there was Joe. He was only about 5'8", dark brown hair and possessed a "five o'clock shadow" by noon. He was very different from anyone I had ever dated. He was fun, and it was innocent.

The first date was a Kansas City Royals baseball game. It was late September and the California Angels were in town. I liked baseball and the home team was quite competitive in the American League. Joe was impressed with my knowledge of baseball and my interest in the game. The courtship had begun. I had absolutely no idea where this was to lead.

We didn't live together. I had my house and a female roommate to share expenses. Joe had a roommate as well. This was "not unusual" for anyone. It made sense during the time when you are first starting out and trying to make ends meet.

We attended various events, had dinner regularly, and became confidants. We still maintained our individuality and kept in contact with our own friends but our worlds were rapidly combining and uniting. We learned more about each other. I found out that not only was he a baseball fan, but he was also a card collector. He started as a young boy and continued into adulthood. He attended "shows" where collectors buy, sell and trade. I was educated into the world of sports memorabilia which included autographs, baseballs, anything "collectible "with "potential value" in the future.

The summer of 1985 was one that lives on in infamy for the Kansas City Royals. The team went to the playoffs, and then eventually to the World Series. I met Joe's dad for the first time attending one of the games. They lived in St. Louis Cardinal territory and were huge redbird fans. They had arrived in Kansas City to be met by a sea of blue opposition. I had met his mother earlier in the year, trying to impress her with veal scaloppini at my home. I don't think I have ever made that meal again.

We were not sexually active at first. It happened, but I really don't remember the first time. What I do remember is him telling me that "he was a virgin" – I was not. To this day, I believe that was his first lie. I was in love, no doubt about that. I had met my soul mate and was ready to finally settle down. We were serious but in looking back on all of this, I now believe that I was definitely more serious about marriage than he ever was. I was blinded by love and not paying any attention to the red flags that were flapping in front of my face like prayer flags in Nepal.

Mutual friends invited Joe over to "look at diamonds". Annie told Joe to pick out the biggest rock he could afford and not to let me get away. The proposal came, actually while we in bed making love, but he wanted to ask somewhere else so that we wouldn't have to tell our (someday) children the "real story". Again, replace fact with a fabricated story – this was to be my future. I wasn't seeing it.

The beginnings of our marriage were everything I had ever imagined in a marriage. We made love often and had what could be stated as a perfect relationship. Our first child, a son, was born about a year and a half into our marriage with a daughter to follow twenty-two months after that. I was thirty-one years of age when our first child was born and continued my life in the corporate world. It was only after the birth of my second child that I decided to quit my job and become a stay-at-home mom. An "unexplained bruise" at our daycare involving our daughter led to my decision to be a full time mom. I would never regain those years – you only get one chance. This would become a pivotal moment in my relationship with Joe. In what appeared to him to be a rash decision had been tearing away at me for two years. He did not have control over my feelings and never would.

The kids each started pre-school at a local Catholic school and I got involved in volunteer organizations. I loved giving my time to help others and received so much more in return. I participated in all the kids' events and was "living the American dream". I had the house in suburbia, the dog, the cat and two kids. What more could a woman want?

Joe's life started into a separate direction. He immersed himself into work, changing jobs, and going into a partnership with others to form a business. It was an unbelievable opportunity to really reap the benefits of his education and to secure a nest egg for ourselves into the future. Appearances however were very deceiving.

Joe had frequent bouts with migraine headaches; he had muscle spasms so severely that one New Years Eve he ended up in a hospital emergency room. He was nauseated frequently, took loads of Tylenol for his aches and pains despite my warnings. I never thought much about his illnesses but did feel like he regularly was "sick" on the weekends when it was "family time".

Occasionally when we went out with other couples, Joe would spend a great deal of the conversation talking with the woman while almost ignoring the man. I had really strange feelings about this and would mention it to him during the car ride home. I would in turn receive a reply that would point out something I had done "wrong" and that would be the end of the conversation.

Our lovemaking became more infrequent. I could easily substantiate this because we were the parents of two young children. Yes, I was tired and would go to bed earlier than he. I got up earlier in the morning, made breakfast and packed lunches for school, drove the carpool, put out the trash and threw a load of laundry in the washer all before I did anything for myself. Joe in turn, would awaken and take care of himself. I laugh when I think back - he could spend much more time in the bathroom than me. Who had the luxury of time in the morning?

Joe was never much of a social person. Our friends were my friends. He "piggybacked" on my relations. He only brought one "couple" into our marriage. The rest of his friends were single and he had one friend who he laughingly explained "was gay". He spent a great deal of time at work but this was not unusual for a man in his late 30's climbing the corporate ladder. Then it all changed. The year was 1999.

He told me he was "depressed". What does that mean? I am a "glass half full person", full of hope and aspirations. How can a person be depressed when absolutely everything is going your way? You have two beautiful children, a wife, and a wonderful future with a progressive company. What is wrong?

Then I found the pictures on the computer. There was Todd, Dan, Dave and who knows – naked, that's all I really remember. I really wasn't checking up on him, I was vigilant in protecting my children from the evils of the Internet. It wasn't them – it was Joe. Furious, I headed to his office and yanked him outside to "talk" in the car. My question was simple – "Are You Gay"? I was met by the response – "No". "But why were you looking at porn pictures?" I countered. "Because I was bored", he replied. I believed him. I was married to him and I trusted.

He lost his job two months later, spiraled into a deep depression and, thrust me into a world I never had any connection with before – psychiatrists, and psychologists. He was prescribed antidepressants and anti-anxiety medications.

Little pills with smiley faces appeared in our medicine cabinet. We went to psychologists to talk about our relationship. We weren't communicating well according to Joe. I felt the same. Communication is a two way street. I asked questions but was met with nothing. I mean absolutely nothing. No emotion, no reply, just nothing. It made me furious. I was angry, no doubt about it. I would make him mad just to get something out of him. When a loved one is depressed you support them, at least that is what all the literature tells you.

He lost interest in just about everything. The baseball cards were in the closet and he simply didn't care about them anymore. He was sad that our children were growing up. He had no interest in anything and sex was non existent. You see, those little smiley face pills make you feel better, but a major side affect is that a man has difficulty in achieving an erection. So it is how the lack of lovemaking was explained to me.

"For Better or For Worse", that is the vow. I am an honest woman, committed to the relationship and cemented in the ideals of marriage. One does not leave a marriage because your spouse is suffering from mental illness – plain and simple – you just don't.

It did get worse. The illnesses, neck pain, shoulder pain, sleep apnea, acid reflux disease. He would take more medications, utilize a breathing machine at night, and visit a chiropractor regularly. Physicians explained that regular exercise would help as physical activity alters brain chemistry and promotes a feeling of well being. So Joe joined the gym.

Joe visited the gym occasionally at first. He would ride a bike and use a treadmill. He said "he felt better". I was all for that. I had gut feelings that the illnesses were psychosomatic. What did I know; I wasn't educated in the mental health arena or the medical field. His "visits" to the gym became much more frequent.

Our fights and arguments escalated, the years melted together. I felt like I was living in a toilet bowl. I actually used that visual with a counselor. I was holding onto to two kids and myself while Joe was constantly flushing us away.

Then the changes in me began.

I couldn't "help" him anymore. I needed to focus on "ME" and the two children that I had brought into the world. My love and admiration for my husband was dying. I tried to communicate my feelings with Joe but was met again with nothing or a complete reversal of the conversation which would usually result in him blaming me for something. A person's soul is visible through their eyes and Joe was dead – he didn't care. Divorce ran through my head and became a secret desire. I knew in my heart that "happily ever after" was not going to happen in my life with this man. Then came my epiphany.

I was away on my own, sitting on a log overlooking a beautiful lake on an early morning in June. I was much happier alone than I was with Joe. I was afraid of my feelings and wanted to know "why". Upon my return home, I separated my head from my heart and began my discovery into his secret life. I checked his cell phone and wrote down numbers. I checked his "gym bag" and the trunk of his car. My findings were shattering. I found condoms, lubricants, handcuffs and various gay literature. I vomited in the back yard of my home for two hours. It was true and my fears were met. He had been lying for years and I simply did not want to believe it.

I kept my knowledge secret for five months as I was preparing myself for the long road ahead of me. I confronted Joe in November and again, six years later, asked the question, "Are you gay"? I again was met by defiant eyes and the answer "no". It was amazing, he could still lie. This time I was ready with names, addresses, phone numbers all burned into my memory. All he said was "It's over". I still do not know to this day what that meant – the secret or his marriage, I really didn't care.

He finally said" I'm Gay" two days before Christmas. In hindsight, it probably was the best present ever – I had an answer. We told the kids, now 18 and 16 that we were going to divorce and despite his protests, I told them that their dad was gay. My anger and hatred were hidden well when the message was delivered and I spoke of education and knowledge of homosexuality. I never wanted my husband to wonder "if" I told them or "what I had said". At the same time, I never wanted my kids to come to me someday and ask why I wasn't truthful to them. It was all out in the open now and the healing would begin.

There is no happy ending and the end is still evolving.

The divorce has been filed; we separated five months ago. Every day is a new day and I am surrounded by a supportive family and many friends. I do not have shame or guilt, and although my confidence has definitely been shaken, it is still high. I will be a better woman, mother, sister and friend because of this ordeal.

The ball cards and all the sports memorabilia – yes—they came out of the closet too! They have been stored for 16 years in the best closet in the house. I cleaned the closet and am using it for other storage.

To those who have tread this path before me, thank you for helping me along the way. To those who are just starting your journey, take my hand.

Story 21: My Life Fell Apart - Auggie

Hi, my name is Lynn P., and I am married to a gay man, but that is not how it started. I was 14 and I had lost my father when I was 10, and I very much longed for male attention. I started high school and met Jon. He was 17 and cute. I made a move and he ignored me and I tried a little harder. We became friends.

At age 15 we were dating behind my mother's back. She had remarried a minister, and I was not allowed to date at that point. I was taught that you did not have sex until you were married, and then you stayed with the man you married.

Jon hung out with his male friends a lot. He did not want me to join them, and I was jealous. When he was with me, he started asking me to go all the way and I kept saying "no", but if he said if I loved him, I would. On my 16th year and his graduation, I had sex and that started a lustful relationship, as he always was coming on to me. How was I to know at this age that he did men? My mother never explained anything about sex, but Jon taught me and taught me well.

At this time he was called into the service to Alaska in the Air Force where there were all men living in a remote sight, but why should I worry? No women, Right? Little did I know what was going on. He used to send me pictures of him in his underwear that other guys took. No, I never thought about that.

In 1970 when he was on leave we got married and went on the honeymoon. Everything seemed normal, and I was happy until the next day he disappeared without saying anything about leaving. He was gone for some time and on his return, I asked about his absence and he said he was nowhere. I left it at that not wanting to start a fight. After the honeymoon we packed to move to Myrtle Beach, South Carolina. We had a two bedroom apartment, and it seemed so big and so far away from home. I was alone all day while Jon was on the base.

I thought a child was the answer, but Jon did not like that Idea. But I kept on until I got my way. We had sex every which way—almost. I got pregnant and 12 weeks into my pregnancy, he said he was going to North Carolina to visit a old buddy from basic training. I did not want him to leave me alone as I was having morning sickness all day. It was Thanksgiving, as I remember watching the Macy's Day Parade alone and being scared. I missed him so, and then he got home, but guess what? He brought his friend Ron home with him to visit a while. Again I had no idea or suspicions. It was an old buddy. I fed both of them even though I was the one that should have been waited on. Finally Ron went home but not until Jon took him home.

We had our first child, and Jon was not much of a father. He would have nothing to do with her. My mother came down from Indiana to help out. We remained in Myrtle Beach until 1973 when we moved into mom's house while looking for our own place. Jon was going out without me and said he was going to his brothers or moms. I was okay with this. One day Mom came in and said, "Lynn, I think Jon is Gay!" I didn't want to hear what she had just said. I got angry with her and said, "Why did you say that?" She said that she had seen his car at a well know gay man's house several times. I was appalled.

On Jon's return Mom was not home and I questioned him and he said I must be crazy. Then he started to cry and said, "Don't do this to me!" I asked "WHAT! He said every since he was young people accused him of being gay. I felt sorry for him and dropped the subject. My mistake as I look back. Again I did not want to start anything.

We found a home, and Jon was always going somewhere. I would ask where and he would always say, "Nowhere." I knew he was lying to me about something, but I did not know what and I never thought anymore about what Mom said that day. He had sex with me at frequent times and that was fine. One day he came home with case of genital crabs. I asked, "Where did you get them?" He replied, "From a toilet seat I guess."

Jon was working nights at a factory, and they had a man they called "Paula" whose real name was Paul. Jon talked about the hassles Paul went through. I should have started to put things together, but I didn't. How stupid. Next it was vaginal infections occurring all the time, but I thought there was something wrong with me. He did not change his clothes in front of me, but then I found out he had a swollen testicle and purulent drainage from his penis. He went to the doctor and when he returned, I asked what him what the doctor said. Jon told me the doctor just gave him a shot. In retrospect, I think it was a STD.

Jon was a factory union president and had to make out-of-town trips. I was never allowed to go. By 1976, I had another little girl, and I had to be there for my children. I just let him go out, but I was upset as he was going out a lot. I thought there might be another woman. I had gained some weight with the new baby, so I lost weight to be more attractive to him. It didn't work.

In 1979 we moved to Southwest Florida. My dad died in 1980, and mom got sick and died of cancer in 1984. Life seemed to go on. I went back to school as I felt there was something wrong, and I needed a career just incase. I became a cardiac nurse in the local hospital. I started to work 12-hour shifts.

Jon was working for his brother and would say he was working late. I found out he was not. I questioned him and he said he stopped to see a friend. I went to church one Sunday and the pastor wanted to see my husband. He said he would not go see him. I thought this was strange. So I went to the pastor and he said that one of the men in the church confessed to having sex with men and Jon was involved too.

I met Jon at the door and he was quiet. He had been let go from his job. I asked why and he told me that his brother was down sizing. I asked his brother who claimed that he had seen the company truck where it should have not been. I confronted

Jon and he denied anything and said I must be imagining things. I was so upset.

How could I be imagining things? But he had me snowed. He then said he loved me and please don't leave him and started to make love to me. One day I was in the car and found a magazine under the seat. It was a gay pornography magazine. It was as if he wanted to be found out now. Still he denied being gay or ever being with a man. He said the book which he found along the road was just curiosity. I could not handle this and went to a hospital in California as far away as possible. I was to have a phone conference and Jon refused. When I returned, Jon had a limo waiting with wine and roses just like nothing had happened. I was furious.

The years were passing by and I was going to a counselor. Jon would not go as he said he didn't need to go to one. Then one day I got a call. Jon had donated blood and it was tested and showed syphilis and I had to go to the health department and get tested also. They drilled me about my sex life and I told them I had only been with one man, my husband. I questioned my husband again about being gay and he denied it again, but said he had been with men since age 14. Most of them were strangers. Now I knew why there were all those STD's.

I went to work and tried to work, but I could not function. Then I guess I broke. I don't remember much, only that I ended up in the hospital with some kind of breakdown. I was going to leave. We had been married 25 years now. I became a self abuser and suicidal for several years. He said everything would change and it was all over. I saw no way out. I lost my job from the breakdown. I could not function.

I still am suspicious even though he says it's over and we have not had much sex since that day. Now not at all as he wanted to always get it from a position similar to having sex with a man. I feel I can't leave him, and I do still love him although he is still a liar. I can't trust him and I live with fear.

So why do I stay? I got tested for AIDS and I am fine. Jon was tested for life insurance. He is okay. I just live a lonely life. I feel my whole life was lost and that my marriage died a long time ago. I have no marriage, no job, no sex, no life. If I had just not let him manipulate me into thinking I was stupid—imagining things, convincing me he loved me and I needed him. I am living inside his closet. No one knows about his past. He is well known in the community, but they just don't know his past/present lifestyle. Gay is Gay and he's not going to change. I have come to grips with that. I just can't leave; I don't know why. I have been married 36 years this year. My girls are 30 and 35. They do know now after I wrote a book. Jon doesn't know they know. I finally told my family so they would not be surprised if I should get brave and get out some day. I have support now and that is good. I am just depressed. My grandchildren are my life now, not my husband.

Story Number 22: The End of Life As I Knew It by: Cathy A.

I was brought up in a warm, happy family that showed affection and love easily. My parents had a very happy marriage and were good examples for me. Jim's family was not as close as mine and didn't show affection as easily but they did love each other. Both of us were brought up with good, solid morals and I realize now grew up in very sheltered lifestyles.

The only exposure I had to homosexuals was having had two obviously gay male friends in high school who hung around me and the rest of our "group" of fifteen or so guys and girls. To be honest, they may have been obviously gay to my friends but were only very effeminate to me. It was understood these were good friends but not dating material, yet I didn't really know a lot about different sexual preferences. Jim's only exposure that I know of was his family had friends that had a gay son. Early in our marriage we did know two young couples who divorced because the husbands were gay. We thought "how sad" and never dreamed it would ever happen in our lives.

Jim and I met in college in 1966 and married in 1968, at age 19. Neither one of us were at all "experienced" when we married. I had dated only a few guys and he really hadn't dated at all. Because of our upbringing and maybe the fact that I was born Catholic and he changed to Catholicism before we even dated, neither of us had "been with" anyone before. We were the first grandchildren to be married on both sides and we had a large formal wedding in the Catholic Cathedral of my hometown.

When we first met I wasn't really attracted to Jim but I didn't want to hurt his feelings either. He continued to pursue me until I finally noticed him. It was obvious that he liked me very much and he treated me like a queen. He didn't give up and eventually grew on me. After awhile we were inseparable and very much in love.

In the early years of our marriage we were a very close and happy couple except for his lack of interest in the sexual part. When we did make love it was wonderful but it was very seldom. I didn't think that was normal but I attributed it to "the way he was brought up" and the lack of intimacy I sensed in his family. In fact, I remember us joking about the birth of our second child having almost been an immaculate conception! We were best friends and I never questioned his love for me.

Our lack of sex was frustrating and puzzling to me. Sometimes in my frustration I'd even ask him if he was gay. I continued to ask him this same question every once in a while through the years, out of concern and confusion rather than anger. I remember wondering *why he didn't get mad* when I asked this question. He'd just responded with "no, don't be ridiculous" and the subject was dropped. Many nights I cried myself to sleep wondering why he wasn't interested in making love. It was frustrating and very demeaning to me. When this happened my self confidence would plummet and I would wonder what was wrong with me. I knew our sometimes sexless marriage was not the way it was supposed to be. That should have been a very big sign but in those days it wasn't to me. When Jim finally went to the doctor about this problem, we were told his testosterone level was low. For a while he took hormone shots, until he'd get tired of taking them. This cycle continued throughout our marriage.

In our thirties, Jim had serious problems with severe clinical depression. He even had several suicide attempts which were devastating to all of us. I attributed his lack of interest to his depression, the effects of his medication. His depression had a strong impact on us, our children and our marriage. I naively tried to make the best of a marriage with the man I loved whose depression constantly overshadowed our marriage. I continued to believe that except for his depression we had a good, strong, solid marriage and nothing would take us away from each other. I thought only death from his suicide possibly could cut short our life together or keep us apart.

Thirty seven years after our wedding, life as I knew it came to an end. I happened to watch a show on Oprah about straight wives and gay husbands. As I watched the show by myself, many of the things hit home, but I still in no way thought my husband was really gay! That evening because it had been a long time since we'd made love, I teasingly told him about the show and the things that seemed similar to our relationship. His response was, as he had told me many times before, "don't be ridiculous, I am not gay!"

A couple of nights later, I was painting ceramics, and he called me in to the kitchen to talk. I'll never forget the date; it was sixteen months ago and only four days before our thirty-seventh anniversary. He told me he hadn't been honest with me when I'd told him about the show on television. He simply said to me, "I *am* gay". He said he'd only recently discovered it and not long ago told his psychiatrist. Those words felt like daggers in my heart, and while I burst into tears, I didn't fully understand yet how much this confession would shatter my life, affect the lives of our daughters, and shock our friends and family.

As he tried to explain his feelings, it was like he was talking to a close friend, not a wife; he continued to tell me things about his homosexuality, his discoveries, and his thoughts. He talked about what he dreamed of doing and how. He also said that what I'd previously called his obsession with a man at his office was really a crush on this man. He told me about the gay porn on his computer and how he waited until I was gone shopping or out of town so he could enjoy it. He admitted to having gay magazines. He even told me how much he loved me, had "never really cheated" on me, and how he wanted us to stay together. He wanted for me to agree he could "see men" on the side. He actually thought this was possible. The trauma of listening to his feelings as they poured out was honestly the worst I've ever been through in my life. I'm sure he'll never understand that conversation would forever be engraved in my mind.

To this day I cry when I just think about that conversation. I can't really explain the pain I felt; it was like living in a nightmare.

After the initial shock I didn't know what to say or how to act. I'd never felt so alone before. I immediately began my search for books on the subject and I read everything I could get my hands on. I thought knowledge would enable me to understand and to sort out all that I now knew. It helped me get through the days knowing the facts and discovering others, both men and women, had been through this horror too.

I cried for weeks and avoided our daughters and grandchildren. Finally I insisted he tell the girls. They knew something was terribly wrong; they were scared that one of us was going to die and we didn't want to tell them. With both of us in the room, we had them come over separately and Jim told them his news. This devastated both of them, but they acted like they were handling it well. Our oldest daughter is a social worker and has handled it best, even though her heart was breaking.

The youngest one handled it well in front of him, only to fall apart later. She told me she was so shocked she almost passed out. She won't talk about it at all now. For a long time she thought we should stay together but has come to realize that is not possible. I think she thought if she didn't address it, it would go away. Now, she knows it's not going away, but she still doesn't see him much. He's not the big part in her life that he used to be. Our grandchildren are very young and have accepted the separation, but they still ask about it and want to know why Grandpapa doesn't want to live with me anymore. How do we explain this to very young children? The fallout from all of this has been devastating.

Jim remained in our home, sleeping in the guest room only after I insisted, for four long months. Knowing things could never be the same again, and that being together was harder on both of us, he moved to an apartment in the next town.

Throughout all of this, I've been through so many and such strong feelings, both emotional and physical. Shock, being sick to my stomach, anger, hurt, denial, hate, love, compassion and disbelief became part of my life. I felt cheated, used, shame, resentment, and feelings I cannot even describe. These are only some of those emotions that keep cycling through over and over again. While I'd been a very trusting, self-confident and secure person, this shook my trust in the whole human race and even my trust in God. I felt like my world was crumbling around me. I sought the advice of my priest, who helped me understand it was not my fault, and my feelings were normal cycles of grief, of losing someone close to me. He encouraged me to get on with my life since these were matters I had no control over. I honestly believed Jim's death would have been easier for me to cope with.

When I look back now I thought we had a solid, happy marriage, I can see there were warning signs and from what I know now was a lack of normalcy. These last few years, when I felt his affection for me seem to lessen, I felt very lonely and sometimes would even tell him, I felt like he would be perfectly happy to live by himself with just his dogs. He didn't have a need anyone else in his life. I also told him it felt like he loved his dogs more than me and sometimes and it made me jealous. Repeatedly, he would say to me, "Don't be ridiculous, that's not true" and he'd change the subject.

I also told him that his reaction on our 25 anniversary trip was not a reaction of someone in a happy marriage. In a hotel on that special night, afterwards, he just rolled over and said "I can't do this anymore". This hurt tremendously and I cried myself to sleep. When I questioned him the next morning, he told me he didn't know why he told me that, it just came out. Of course later he'd tell me that he didn't mean what he'd said, it had been his depression talking, not his true feelings. Knowing what I know now makes that very debatable. Those were signs I missed.

We were best friends and I knew he loved me. I guess I was not only in love with the man I married, but in love with the way things should have been, not how they had been. I never doubted his love for me; I just didn't know it was not the kind of love it was supposed to be.

He says he didn't know or admit his homosexuality to even himself. That's hard for me to understand because it seems like it's impossible NOT to know. Surely he questioned his feelings as being strange for someone married to a straight wife. How could he not know those feelings, those thoughts, his lack of intimacy, his gay porn were not of a homosexual nature? I think he lied to himself and lied to me for years because he didn't want to be gay and didn't want anyone to know, *not* because he didn't know deep inside what his feelings were.

How sad it is when I think about all of those lies, the cheating he did, even if only in his thoughts. Just how much of our marriage was a lie…how much a cover or a safety net so he could believe things were normal instead of coming clean to himself, his world, our family and mostly to me. I cry my eyes out when I think about this, but I really want to scream and shout to God, to Jim and to the world that it's not fair for him have to have lied to me to protect himself. Jim even told me that I didn't deserve this, and it was his problem, not mine. Why then did he use me…make me suffer from his isolation and the lack of intimacy. Many nights I cried myself to sleep because I didn't understand why he avoided sex with me, turned me down so often and sometimes seemed so distant. He would say the problem was he wanted me to initiate it and so I did and still he turned away and turned down so many, many times.

He should have admitted his being gay years ago, before I gave him the best years of my life. And even if he really did only recently admit it to himself, this late in life he should have left it alone. This marriage should never have happened. He didn't have a right to marry me. Gay men shouldn't marry at all! It is selfish and extremely devastating for a wife to find out years later. Too me, this is the hardest way to end a marriage. It would have been much easier if there was another woman. To know that one day there will be a man taking my place is agonizing.

It's hard for me now, knowing he's happy or at least happier without me, living a different life with different people and very different lifestyles. I do believe, one day I'm going to cross the line out of the past and into the present and future, but it's taking me a long time. After all, it took 37 years to build our marriage, so it's going to take a while for me to put all of this behind me. There are so many wonderful memories I have of our marriage, but it's not those memories that come to my mind these days. It's the ugly memories that take center stage until I can take the road to move on alone. I don't want it to be that way, it just *is* right now. It's unbelievable how fast it can go from loving each other to feeling like strangers. I never dreamed this would happen to us and it's difficult to think about us living separately and never growing old together. NO, I don't want him back like he is now or has been for a long time. I just want my life back, and I want to move forward, but I also want things to be like I thought they were before.

I'm hoping that telling my story will be therapeutic and help me sort through my feelings, as well as warn other women and let them know they are not at all alone. It isn't nearly as rare a situation as one would think. I want to let the world know what trauma and horror happens when a straight wife finds out her husband is gay. I hope writing my story will help me to pick up the pieces in my shattered life and be able to look to the future. I've tried so very hard to let go of the past and I'm told I will one day. I'm already much better, and I'm handling things better now than I did when I first realized my life as it had been before would never, ever be the same again.

I'm trying to throw myself into a job so I can build my life around something different than I have in past times. I've always been a wife, mother, sister, daughter, niece, etc. *Family* defined what my aims and accomplishments were until January 16, 2005, four days before our 37th wedding anniversary when he told me his secret. I realize from therapy and friends that I cannot change the past and should not dwell on it. I am still trying with all of my might to move forward. My daughters, my sister, and my close friends have been as supportive as anyone can be. I would not be where I am today if it had not been for them. I also wouldn't have made it without Bonnie Kaye, our online group, and my therapist. Like my sister says, I've been trying to make sense out of something that doesn't make sense. I believe she is right.

Story Number 23 - My Story – By Paula K.

Wow, I never thought that I would be writing a story like this. At times you think that your life is absolutely perfect and then, BAM, it hits. Not only do you realize that your life is not perfect, but you realize that it has been absolutely shattered and a lot of what you thought it was, was not even true.

My story begins in 1976 when we started dating. My sister's husband was a police officer and my husband was a friend of his. I met him socially through them. I should have been suspicious from the start because we went out once but he didn't ask me out again for almost a year. Even when he did finally ask me out it took coaxing from my brother-in-law. I should have realized that if he were truly interested in me, he would have asked me out sooner. I did date other guys in the meantime, but always held out hope that he would eventually come around.

As I'm recounting my story I keep retyping the phrase "I realize now" or "I should have realized"…I don't want to overuse that word. It seems so obvious now that a lot of what happened between us should have tipped me off. I should have realized so much. We dated, but only saw each other about once a week. He was a new police officer working often and I was still in college and had a full time job. I blamed all of that on why it was that we didn't see each other. I am still very busy now, with social activities, community service, mentoring, family, and hobbies, but for some reason I still have time, almost everyday, for the boyfriend i have now! I guess my point is if being together was important to my boyfriend in back 1976, it would have happened.

We started dating officially in Feb., got engaged in Dec. and married the following August. We did have sex before we were married (he was the only person for me, can't answer for him) but we both lived at home so we basically only had sex in a car…and not often. Again, I blamed that on the fact that we

160

didn't see each other and we lived at home so it wasn't convenient. I thought that maybe when we got married it would change. It didn't. Ok, we didn't have sex in the car anymore, but we didn't have sex all that much. I was young and being sexually inexperienced I just followed his lead.

As time went on, I realized that I really liked having sex and I was (always) very attracted to my husband. I have learned over the last eight years how very sexual heterosexual men are. I didn't know that thirty years ago. I have since had other relationships and those relationships combined with interaction with friends and coworkers I now see that had I been privy to that information I would have been more aware that perhaps something was amiss in my marriage. I know how naive it sounds to say that, but when you live with a man that just doesn't act like that, like men who eat, sleep, drink, think and breathe sex, it's easy to be fooled. He didn't ogle other women. I thought I was lucky for that. He didn't have girlie magazines. Again, what a lucky girl am I.

As time went on I became more interested in sex and more frustrated because he wasn't. It wasn't just the lack of desire on his part, but for other reasons I knew something was wrong. I just didn't get a sense that we were like other couples. I didn't see in us what I saw in them. Couldn't figure it out then, but I knew something was different. Would I have guessed that he was gay? Absolutely not. Never even crossed my mind. Aside from the typical signs, there were other, less obvious signs that I should have noticed. He had anger and I could never figure out where it came from. He would get mad at the smallest of things. Now, I'm thinking, was it just a way to have a fight so he wouldn't have to have sex? Was it because he was living a double life (something i would later figure out) and the stress of that caused the outbursts? I'm no psychologist but it all seems very clear to me now.

After three years of marriage we started our family so that helped occupy my time and not feel sorry for myself. Sorry because I wasn't getting my hand held, wasn't thrown on the bed, wasn't getting much in the way of physical attention. I know it may seem silly, and I probably thought so then, but if you are a couple that has all of that going for you, you wouldn't understand. Try going many years with a partner that just has no interest in you in that way. It's fine if it's mutual, but when it isn't, it's very unsatisfying. We all have a need to be desired. For me, that was the biggest thing. I knew my husband loved me, and still does. I know he would kill or die for me. But once I knew what it was like to be truly desired by someone, I finally knew what I had been missing. Problem was, I still did not yet know why that was missing in my marriage. I did have thoughts that perhaps he wasn't attracted to me, but then, why did he marry me? I also thought that maybe he was having an affair. There was some evidence to that and when I approached him I was told I was wrong.

In my twenties I was raising my toddlers. In my thirties I was back at work. By the time I reached my forties my children were almost grown and I was settled in my career. I think that's why suddenly, at this point in my life, I had more time to think about why I was so unhappy. I was preoccupied before with things that fulfilled my life. I was generally happy with my life, it was my love life that needed help. I look back at a journal that I kept on occasion and some of my entries were very pathetic. How I craved attention from my husband. I never told anyone. How do you tell someone that your husband never wants to be with you? I just figured they would look at me like something must be wrong with ME. That's what I thought, why wouldn't anyone else? I know women are probably not so preoccupied with their love lives, but when you don't really have one, it's a different story. I had the occasional guy flirt with me and sometimes even hit on me but it never phased me because I was married and knew that I shouldn't be interested elsewhere. I also knew how attracted I was to my husband, so even though I was inwardly unhappy, I was not interested in anyone else. At least, not yet...

I could go on for days with the different things that happened in the relationship with my husband. At times I felt like we were more buddies than lovers. We were great as parents together and we had an active social life. We both got along well with each others families, but when it came to intimacy, and not just sexual intimacy, we were truly lacking. I would actually have to seduce him in to having sex. If I just outright asked, it never worked. If I waited for him and set the scene, it sort of trapped him. How can a man, even a gay one, say no when he walks into a room lit with candles, wine poured, wife lying in her sexiest lingerie? I had to do that to ensure I wouldn't get rejected. I would actually calculate when the last time we had sex was. The reason for this was because if I asked too soon I was sure to get shot down. If I waited a while, usually more than a month, I could almost guarantee that I would get a "yes". Even then, it was iffy! How sad is that?

I always heard from girlfriends how their husbands were always after them for sex. I was intrigued. Not because their husbands wanted sex and mine didn't, but because the girls were annoyed at their husbands behavior! It fascinated me. Why would these women not want to be the object of their husband's desire? I guess, when men are constantly craving you, you get tired of it. Who knew? Still I never let on to my secret. Especially now, when I find out that that is the way of the world and my husband was just not like that.

As we were approaching our twentieth anniversary it really made me stop and think about what had transpired over the years. I knew then that I wasn't happy with the way we were and I needed to do something about it. I just wasn't sure what that was. I complained to my friends that this anniversary was all his. He better think of something good. He better make it romantic and special. They all asked if he ever did stuff like that and I said "no", to which they responded that he probably was not going to this time either. Still, I was adamant. I was not going to settle for anything less than spectacular. And yes, even I knew what I was asking was not realistic, it's still how I felt. In the meantime my best friend and her husband were also getting ready to celebrate their twentieth and we decided to do something together. We all went on a cruise. Off the hook again. Someone else planned my vacation and he got a free ride. It was romantic (at least I thought so) and nice. Interesting, though, that a week after we got home, I started having an affair.

In spite of how I had been feeling, I still would have called anyone a liar if they said I was about to embark on an affair. I truly believe in fidelity and wanted to live a long and happy life with just one person. It's just that with that scenario it takes two devoted, honest, sincere people to make that happen. Two people who have a mutual desire for each other. People have affairs for all kinds of reasons, and I'm not saying mine is the best, or to be condoned, but it happened. I'm not proud that it did, nor am I ashamed. It had to happen in order for me to be able to get to the truth-the truth about my marriage.

My husband and I were out with one evening with friends. He left early and I stayed with the gang. He said that someone would bring me home, anyone. He even mentioned the name of the person that would eventually give me a ride. The evening was fun and by the time my husband left I had had a couple of glasses of wine and was probably a little less inhibited than I normally am. I was dancing with a friend, and we were flirting with each other. There is still a question as to who was making the first move. I say it was him, he says it was me! Nevertheless, we didn't go right home that night!

To make a long story short (because this one spans eight years!!!) we started seeing each other. It was very sporadic the first year, seeing each other only about once a month or so, but talking everyday. Everyone knew both of us so we had to be discreet. He was single, but seeing someone, and I was married. I never thought in a million years I would have done something like this, but here I was doing it and not feeling very guilty. Finally, I had what I was missing. It wasn't even just the sex. It's the way a couple interacts with each other in all aspects of their lives. Just the way he talked to me on the phone, the things he would say and how he would say them.

This sounds silly, like I had never had this experience before, but quite frankly, I hadn't. I met my husband at 19. I started dating at 20, engaged at 21 and married by 22. Prior to him, I just dated boys in high school and college. And that's exactly what they were – boys. Now this was a guy that had all the moves and lines. I would be less than honest if I didn't mention that he was a womanizing fool. He had a very long history, and I was familiar with it. Some people, once they were privy to the affair, thought that I must have been naïve for believing him or even being with him at all. Quite the contrary because I think it was the first time I wasn't being naïve at all! I knew what he was like, but didn't really care, at least not in the beginning. He gave me what I was missing in my marriage. Friends and family asked, why him? But my response was "it had to be him". It had to be someone I knew because it's not like I left the house with intent to cheat. I would have never been comfortable with a stranger. It had to be someone that would do what he did, with the wife of a friend. I wasn't looking for everlasting love because I was already married and had that. It was everlasting lust I was looking for. Well, maybe not looking for, but it found me. And I'm very glad it did.

One day I received a phone call from my husband informing me that he knew about the affair and he was leaving. He overheard a conversation on the phone. He was very upset, and I was devastated. How could I have done this to the man I love and promised to be true to? How did I end up here? What is wrong with ME? Eventually people found out, friends and family alike. It's true what they say about how in times of trouble, you know who your friends are. Almost immediately, I was held up to public scrutiny. How could she do that to him? He is such a wonderful, perfect husband. Yeah, I had to endure that for almost five years. In spite of that, I continued to see the other man. My husband and I separated but still were together as a family for the kids.

I'm sure everyone thought I stopped the other relationship, but what they didn't know at the time was that almost as soon as my husband left, information starting coming to me concerning his sexual orientation. I was stunned. A gay friend of mine had posed it as a possibility to me earlier, but I dismissed it as ridiculous. I mean, geez, I was married to the man – if anyone knew, I certainly would! Only now would all of my suspicions about his having an affair, combined with STDs he contracted, and his lack of sexual desire, only now, did it all start to make sense. Even so, it still took me almost two years to confront him. We were separated during that time but I still found it difficult to actually ask him. What if I was wrong? I think the real reason I hesitated was because I knew I wasn't wrong.

I finally got the nerve, but he denied it. He actually dismissed my accusations all together. We remained separated until he found out that I was still seeing the other man. It upset him, and he moved back in. I can only imagine now, that with my revelation, he probably was worried that I wouldn't beg him to come home. In the beginning that was how it was, but once I started processing all of the "gay" information, the begging him to come home stopped.

He was home for six months when I finally had enough. I left one night and didn't tell him where I went. He was very upset. The next day we talked and he confessed. Well, he said, yeah, maybe something happened, but acted like it was no big deal and he still wanted to stay married. Of course, marriage worked for him. He had the perfect life – the perfect wife, the perfect kids, the whole perfect picture. He even had the perfect sex life, it just wasn't with me. But now his perfect wife had an affair and the perfect picture started to fade. Staying married would suit him, but not me. To think of all the times I threw myself at him, now knowing that nothing would have worked. Why on earth would I want to continue to be with a man whom I knew did not desire me? It may have worked for him, living a double life, but my double life didn't work for me.

I wanted to get everything I wanted in ONE man and I knew it was possible. I had enough role models in family and friends. Interesting, but at one time, for over twenty years, my husband

and I were the perfect role models. Others were devastated by the demise of our relationship, and I took the fall. Even when I initially found out about him I didn't tell anyone right away, except for those from whom the information came. I knew that even though I was hurt by what he had done, lead me through a life of deceit. I still felt compassion for the fact that he didn't seem to accept his homosexuality. I helped keep his secret, even thought I was being blamed for everything. I could handle that everyone held me accountable but I wasn't sure he could handle everyone knowing about him.

It took the next three years for the entire process to take place. Eventually people found out about him. There was a time I covered for him, but not anymore. I know you are not supposed to "out" a gay person, but this directly involved me. If asked why I wasn't with my husband anymore I answered the question honestly – "because he is gay"…Why not, it was true. He certainly didn't mind people believing I was the scarlet woman. He didn't do anything to save my reputation. Yet, here I was, protecting him. Uh, it was tiring. Still is.

To some extent, I still protect him. I still feel guilty that he does not live with us anymore. Of course, part of that guilt is because he makes me feel that way. I always get the "poor me" feeling from him. Maybe it's just me. As much as I say I feel guilty for not having his family live with him any more, you have to realize that he had a family a lot longer than he should have, or even that he had a family at all. I'm not trying to sound mean, but he should have never married me. He was able to live a life that he shouldn't have for a very long time and now it's time for me to live the live that I should have lived all of this time.

We finally got divorced, which took five years from the time he first learned of the affair. I was torn, at times, because what would people think? She's leaving him because of sex? I even had people tell me that sex wasn't everything and that a lot of couples didn't have it anymore. It was sentiments like that that made me think. Thankfully, I knew exactly what I wanted. I wanted a completely satisfying relationship with someone. Was it the guy with whom I was having the affair? Certainly not! We lasted for five and a half years, and then another two, albeit two torturous years. The sun rose and set on him at first. He was the first heterosexual man I had ever been with and I thought it was great. Upon dating, and yes, sleeping with other men, I realized he wasn't all that special. He was just a straight guy who knew how to show a girl a good time. What ruined it was that he wasn't faithful. Ever. Oh, he pretended like he was, and at times, I pretended like I believed him. I stopped seeing him for that reason but then six months later called him and continued and on and off again situation. Yeah, situation. I don't even think it was an affair anymore and it certainly wasn't a relationship. I learned a lot, though. Particularly what not to look for in a guy!

So, twenty eight years, and many meltdowns later I am finally a free girl. I got divorced the same month I turned fifty. Who knew I would find myself dating again at that age? But I will say this, fifty is fabulous. I feel less guilty and more confident. Both of those relationships took their toll, but I came out of both of them a very strong person. I love them both for what I learned from them, good or bad. I'm just not IN LOVE with either of them anymore.

This story does have a happy "beginning"...the beginning of a new relationship. I am so happy right now. This guy is terrific, but that's another whole story...*one just waiting to be told!*

Story 24 - A letter to my Ex. By RKA

It's almost a year since we have separated, since I found out about what was lurking deep inside you for so long. You live with someone for 10 years. You think you know him. You seem to know what makes him tick, what makes him happy, what pisses him off, even how he thinks. But you never really seem to know everything about him. Mum once said to me that we all have a secret, a secret we keep from our partners. Yours was way overdue. You should have faced your demons back before you got me and the kids into this. You should have done your "experimenting", soul searching and questioning way before we got married. But now I fall into the "should have, would have, could have." It's done – and there is no turning back.

Back a year ago, you suddenly seemed withdrawn, falling into some sort of dark place that I was not a part of. Suddenly you would use the internet at strange hours of the night and suddenly want to go off for a walk to do some soul searching. When I confronted you with what's going on, you complained that you have no life, you have no space, you have forgotten who you are, that you have stopped doing what you have always liked such as painting, that you have only one drawer at home for your personal things, and the rest has been invaded by the kids and me. There were all sorts of strange remarks. I mean you were always one to complain. You were, and still are, a drama queen, but to say something like, "Maybe I should have never had kids," was totally out of character and alarming.

And suddenly there was this new friend in your life. Up until then, I always let you have space and lots of it, because I also liked my space and needed it. Being the intense person that you are, I was happy when you would go out at night with your friends. But when this new anonymous friend whom you spoke of and had this glowing look in your eyes appeared, I felt something was just not quite right. Suddenly you were talking of having a business with this guy who just seemed to inspire you because he was into hulticulture…My G-d. I tried to be practical, asked questions on who is he, what's he about, what's he like, his knowledge of business. You sold me a story which just did not add up on how he is a student that has this magic about him and everyone likes and …that he MAY be gay. Living in Sydney (Australia), I did the math and soon gathered that he is living with his boyfriend.

Meanwhile you were telling me how you needed to get away to straighten yourself out. I was all for it until you said he was coming with you. Again you covered it up by saying you had asked your brother and another couple of mutual friends but no one wanted to come.

So I confronted you. Which straight guy suddenly befriends a gay guy and becomes all googly eyed at him? Still I let you go and you came back all confused. What's amazing is how we can fool ourselves. How we chose not to believe even though the puzzle does not add up – all the bells are ringing, all the red lights are flashing – but no – we chose not to believe.

I, in the meantime, spent the weekend freaking out and picking up smoking all over again. Teary eyed, I was mashing the story back and forth. On your return, you were quiet and dropped a bomb shell at me. You revealed to me that you were raped back seven years ago when we were in Bolivia together. That threw me totally off course. I really did not expect that. However as the week progressed, your moods were hopping from extreme happiness to total withdrawal. You went in for eye surgery to have the laser done. You were sedated for the next few days. I checked your sms and intercepted some words that were a bit obscure.

Eventually I just confronted you and asked if you have issues with your sexuality. You finally admitted the unforgivable.

From that day I went into complete vertigo. What the hell happened? I thought we were happy. I thought any thing could be overcome if there is enough love. What did I know? Looking back at it now, I can see the denial and shock stages I went through. I still believe that if one wants to hard enough, those desires can be overcome. Despite what I have heard from people, all the scientific information I have read has no direct linkage to genetic mutation. I do believe that there is over expression of hormones, of certain proteins that are more evident in gays than straights. I do believe that the psychology and the life experience have a lot to do with it. The thing is what difference does it really matter now?

Initially, I was trying to "bargain" with you and myself. Trying to get you to fight, telling you that even though you feel that way does not make you gay. Just like other men may eye other women and vice versa, you find the men attractive, so what's the big deal? Anyway, we are all human, regardless of what sex we are. In Eastern Europe the porno stars in gay movies don't call themselves gay – but rather they have sex with who ever they find attractive. It's our society to blame that we categorized everything. I even dragged you to a rabbi to get a blessing.

I read this, and I feel so stupid. I don't blame myself, but rather I am astonished on how one would make any excuses, just not the truth.

You moved out pretty much immediately. You had the nerve to say that I was the one who threw you out rather than trying. It's amazing how you tried to manipulate the situation, saying that had I been more intuitive to you, got my family to not interfere so much in out life, paid you more attention, you would have not gone there.

I did not fall for all of this – I told you that I would have done anything to save the relation ship – as long as I could. I even moved to another country. I didn't even realize you were not happy; in fact, you never said you were not. You still don't. Months later I actually think it was a combination of your falling for this guy, you getting bored of the same "fish and chips" you had at home. Life got too hectic with the three young children, and you just could not handle the pressure, so you opened the Pandora box. Someone once said to me that when we feel trapped we look for whatever makes us happier- so you did- you started exploring the dark side in you.

You helped me get to the angry stage very quickly, bypassing the remorse and the regret as you became very selfish. All you cared about was yourself, and how much money you would get out of our break up, how the kids irritated you, yet you threatened to take them away.

My luck is that I am who I am and I know myself unlike you. So for me it was like "just try me." I actually surprised my self on how I was not getting aggressive but rather reacted very defensively. I think it had to do with the fact that there are 3 kids involved. I initially went and found any literature I could about this. I found this amazing website in the states, run by an amazing woman named Bonnie, which helped me understand and realize I am not alone. Through her, I met another local lady whom I have never met in person, but has given me so much support and understanding.

Our kids never saw us fight when we were together. We never really did. We had a great relationship which many others would envy. We worked, played, and had lots of fun together. Our friends were so shocked to hear that we split up. My close girlfriend actually said that if they ever imagined us breaking up it would have come from me. Many have asked me how I could stand being with you – being such a winger and a sulker. At least now I don't have to listen to that.

We run a business together and that's really frustrating. I feel like I am, carrying the whole burden on my own. This is where it's now really pissing me off. You leave, you have a good time, you are looking after yourself and looking great – partying all night, have the kids a couple of times a fortnight, and have all your bills paid. I am even making it easy for you by not disowning you (that would be the bullet for you as you always wanted to be accepted and I will hold this is my joker). I look ragged and tired, and I am becoming the witch from hell because I am so exhausted. I struggle financially as our expenses have gone through the roof and our income has decreased (you being in the clouds and me having to try and carry everything on my own) Its really difficult to start all over again from that perspective. I am yearning to start something else, to have a new beginning, a new career, a new life, and possibly even a new love.

I feel like I have come a long way since a year ago. I know I am not out of the loop yet and I still have a long way to go but I think the worst (at least of the shock) has passed. The challenge of how the children will cope is one of my main concerns. Our eldest, being 8 is like 15. She has always been a more complex and highly intelligent child. For her, when we initially told her of the break up, it didn't take her long to figure that a split may lead to a divorce. I was astounded how as an 8 year old she seems to know so much. Initially I was dumbfounded and got very upset when she would ask me whether we would get back together. So I said I did not know. As time progressed, I would answer differently. I said that you had a lot of issues you had to deal with, and that these issues should have been dealt with many years ago, They make it very difficult to live together as a husband and wife. She would occasionally attack me, say that the reason you left was because my family never liked you (nice one...) This is when I started putting my foot down and not covering for you so much any more. Why should I? I am the one who was lied to, I was the one who had to hold it together while you pranced around, behaving like an immature baby.

I made it clear to my kids that I never wanted any of his to happen-ever.

I never thought it would happen. When you get married, and give each other your vows, when you stand under the Chuppa (Jewish canopy tradition) and make a covenant with each other and G-d, when you have children – and by G-d, three children, well all of that should stand for something. I explained that of course this is a tragedy. Of course this is something I never expected to happen. But it did. Without telling them the full reason, which is very difficult to hold back, I basically had to explain that sometimes in life shit happens. This is a very bitter lesson for such children. But we are still friends (even though I sometimes still wan t to kill you) and that we love the kids very much. When I saw the look on Gabi's face, I hugged her and she said how upset she was feeling. I asked why and she said, "Well does that mean daddy does not love you any more?" I said, "Well, he loves me in a different way…". How tragic is that?"

But you know what? I refuse to spend my life in bitterness. I am willing to stop questioning why-why you are what your are. Stop making the excuses. I want to carry on. I want to look forward to what is coming. It's like our lives are a train. People board the train, come on, and get off, some stay for five minutes, some stay for years. Some who stay for a few minutes may impact our lives forever, and some may be with us forever but have little impact on us. You boarded my train 10 years ago and now its time for you to get off. You are clearing your way for the next person – whoever or whatever it may be. I remember how for the first few months I was aching and praying that I will get to the point where it no longer hurts. Now the pain has subsided, but what remains are the pieces that have to be mended. When I see an older couple who has gone through thick and thin my heart aches. This has always been my dream, and I was robbed of it.

So here I am almost a year later. I am still standing and I will survive this. And get stronger. Tomorrow will come, the sun will shine and life will continue.

And who knows? Maybe I got the monkey off my back…

Story 25 - Teacher, Lover, Jailer by Veronica M.

I met my husband when I was 12 and he was 30. We became sexually involved when I was 25. I bore him a child at 35. Now I am 40. I left him three weeks ago.

It is hard for me to know where to start in explaining the past 28 years, so I'll begin at the beginning. A few weeks into my career as a seventh grader, my English teacher, whom I'll call Mr. Mori, assigned the class an autobiographical speech. He used himself as an example and told us of his early memories, of his mother's death when he was four, and of how all photos of her and dolls she had made for him were destroyed. The tale of that early tragedy struck me. I had already become fond of Mr. Mori, and I suddenly felt a great desire to assuage this pain and loss. I had no idea I would spend half a lifetime trying unsuccessfully to understand and comfort this man.

My terrible crush on Mr. Mori continued after entering high school. My high school was lousy and my parents frequently fought. During my sophomore and junior years, Mr. Mori, myself, and three boys (I'll call them Raj, Hector, and Sutu) fell into an informal, regular social group, which we uncreatively called, "The Group." We played poker and Risk, talked about movies and books, debated, etc. It was kind of a suburban version of the Dead Poets' Society. After awhile The Group gradually fell apart. Mr. Mori spent more time with Hector, and Mr. Mori finally told me to get lost, which hurt but didn't surprise me. I knew I was overly attached to him.

Later I found out there was an additional reason that Mr. Mori wanted me out of the way. Hector, who was 17 at the time, confided in me that Mr. Mori told him he wanted to go to bed with him. Hector rejected the offer, but felt pressured and confused. I was furious—angry that Mr. Mori had taken advantage of a malleable, underage kid, but also jealous, and guilty for feeling jealous of my friend. Mr. Mori's actions were a crime, but Hector's mother told Mr. Mori that if he got therapy she would not press charges. He did two or three sessions, but years later he told me that he did not take the therapy very seriously. I was sure I would be angry at him forever. But for some reason I have found it possible to forgive him things I would not forgive others. After a couple of years, I reconnected with Mr. Mori and we visited sporadically.

By this time I had entered college and had begun my first sexual relationship, with another student seven years my senior. Though the relationship had its share of problems and ended a few years later, the young man was a kind person and a gentle, skilled lover. The wonderful sexual education he gave me proved to be a lifesaver later.

During my college years, I would write Mr. Mori occasionally and visit him when I came home to see my parents. During those years, I gradually became aware that Mr. Mori regarded himself as bisexual. By about 1990 I knew that he had been attracted to or infatuated with at least five males, and made unsuccessful overtures to two of them, both of them from The Group (the aforementioned Hector, as well as Raj, who had come out as a homosexual a couple years before).

By 1991, I was on a first-name basis with Mr. Mori, whom I will now refer to as Yukio, which is not his real name. He suggested I accompany him on a trip to Costa Rica. I assumed his feelings toward me were completely platonic, since at that point he presented himself as gay. During the trip, I felt the resurgence of my old feelings for him, which was rather excruciating. Towards the end of the trip, he expressed sexual desire for me, and our relationship began then as a no-strings-attached liaison.

I should have realized that it's not healthy to be get involved with someone if you are in love with him, and all he really wants is sex, but I did it anyway. I should mention that early on, the "sex" was really only heavy petting; Yukio was not able to maintain an erection until several months into the relationship.

After we returned from our trip, Yukio said that since he was trying to figure himself out sexually, he might have sex with men or with other women. I went along with that, though as far as I know he never actually did step outside of our relationship. Looking back, I can see that I deluded myself with a terrible mixture of wishful thinking, desperation, and lust, mortared together with something halfway between compulsion and true love.

After a few months or so, Yukio told me that he didn't think he was gay, and that he thought his homosexual feelings had been part of a "delayed adolescence" that was now over. I was still so desperate for his love that I accepted the notion he had miraculously become straight. I left my life and friends in the city and moved back to my hometown. I figured it would become clear within a year or two whether or not the relationship would work, and if it didn't I would move back to the city.

After seven years passed, I knew I had to resolve things one way or the other. The relationship had become like an addiction for me: I was habituated to it, but getting no real pleasure out of it and feeling crippled by it. Since the relationship had been established as a no-strings operation, I initially didn't see the point of bringing up marriage.

My mother encouraged me to talk to him, saying that I should at least give him an option one way or the other. I kept recalling the loss of his mother and all the pain other females had caused him. I went around in circles, trying to decide: leave outright, or give him a choice. Finally I went with the latter option, and we decided to get married. At this point, I was still convinced he was straight. The first few years of our marriage went surprisingly well, given its shaky underpinnings. As before our marriage, our intimate life was limited in many ways (for example, oral sex was completely off-limits), and I always perceived a certain "ick" factor for Yukio in dealing with my body, but Yukio was nearly always enthusiastic about basic intercourse. I wrote off the sexual shortcomings to his repression and decades of bachelorhood, and contented myself with what he was able to provide sexually.

One day in March of 2004, I sat down at the family computer to go online. As I had for several previous days, I used my husband's login since the software on my side of the computer had been acting up. The day before I had seen an interesting financial website I wished to revisit, so I hit the "History" function on the browser. I suddenly saw the names of gay porn sites my husband had been viewing over the previous several days. It took a minute to absorb what I was looking at. I felt like I couldn't breathe. Even now, several years later, my pulse rate goes up and my chest feels heavy recalling the moment. It felt like a nightmare.

I realized I had to say nothing and watch his activity for a few days to determine whether or not this was just experimentation. It was a terrible week. My daughter was three-and-a-half, and somehow I managed to not break down in front of her. Some days, I sang almost continuously because it was the only way to keep the tears at bay. Little things that I had brushed off over the years came rushing back to me. For example, I recalled that he told me, after we found out I was pregnant with a girl, that he was relieved it wasn't a boy. He also said from time to time that he thought society in general tended to overreact in proscribing sexual relationships between adults and teenagers in general, and between men and teenaged boys in particular.

Over the course of a week, he visited about a half-dozen gay porn sites per day. During the whole week he only visited one or two sites with naked women. I confronted him, convinced our marriage was over. He told me he had been experiencing a lull in his libido and wanted to see if this would help. He told me all kinds of pleasant things to get me calmed down. Then he told me various things that I had been doing wrong that contributed to his dissatisfaction: being disorganized and a bad housekeeper, "trying to wear the pants" in the family, being negative, being too close to my own family, etc. Then we made love, and he was more passionate with me than he had been in some time. I came away from that conversation convinced it had been my fault that Yukio felt attracted to males again.

I spent the next year furiously improving myself: I lost weight, took vitamins to restore my energy, got more organized, and became more positive. In the course of the year, my family and friends noticed the changes and complimented me. Yukio did not seem to notice. At one point I fished for compliments, and he briefly acknowledged I made some good changes, then went on to point out how awful I had been before. I felt really mad. Then I decided to take it as a challenge. I would just keep getting better and better until he would wake up one morning and say, "How did my wife turn into this amazing woman?"

Our intimate life at this point was not very good. I was finding it difficult to get enthused about being with someone I felt was hypercritical. A couple times I tried to introduce new, pleasant activities, but was met with amiable neutrality or outright rebuffs rather than the lusty enthusiasm I'd hoped for. I tried encouraging him to be more affectionate with me outside of the bedroom, but he said he was too tired. I did not accept this, because I was asking for tenderness, not acrobatics.

To be fair to him, I should add that foreplay wasn't non-existent, but that what foreplay there was, was rough and mechanical, like I was a car he was trying to start. I had had enough experience with my previous lover that I knew this was not the way a man reacts when he is truly turned on by a woman's body, even a woman with whom he has been sleeping for years. Had I still completely believed he was straight, I could have written our difficulties off to boredom and fatigue. But the memory of his gay porn viewing remained.

In January of 2005, Yukio unilaterally decided that we should sell our home. He had purchased it before our marriage and was within his rights, but it was a blow to me because I loved the rural setting. However, the aging house and acreage were a lot of work, and Yukio had become increasingly irritated by noise produced by the back neighbors. I was very sad and angry, and stopped having sex with Yukio, but I told myself that I would get over this eventually and that my affection for him would return. I had forgiven him so much in the past that I assumed I would forgive this too. What I did not realize at the time was that after the gay porn incident the year before, the marriage had become like a vase full of cracks. It only needed a couple of strong taps to shatter completely. And the first tap had just occurred.

Two months later, I traveled to the city to attend an aunt's funeral. It was the first time I had been away from Yukio and my daughter for more than one night. I stayed with my sister, and I quickly realized that being away from Yukio felt very good, as though a weight had been taken off me, even though I felt sad about my aunt's death. I also visited some old friends whom I hadn't seen in some time, and I found that, contrary to Yukio's criticisms of my social skills, I actually could interact with others in a lighthearted, enjoyable manner.

I told my sister about these observations, as well as the gay porn incident. At last I had broken my silence, and it was a relief to finally tell another human being what I had bottled up. I began to entertain the idea that my husband was a repressed homosexual who was manipulating me into believing his dissatisfactions were my fault.

Three days after I returned, I went to a previously-scheduled gynecological check-up. I had been on great terms with my OB/GYN nurse since my pregnancy five years before. I explained my situation to her, and she was extremely supportive. "Make sure he addresses your concerns," she said, and proceeded to test me for all the STDs. Fortunately the tests all came up clean.

Over the next few months, I continued to keep myself at a distance from Yukio. I still had sexual desires for him, but confined the sexual activity to heavy petting. I was determined not to have intercourse with him again until I felt I was on safer psychological ground with him, because I knew that once I resumed full relations, I would to some degree believe anything he said, even if the sex was lousy.

Gradually, I came to see how deeply Yukio controlled me. He rarely put me down outright, but he encouraged my self-doubts. I realized that besides cultivating my social insecurities, he also discouraged me from visiting friends who didn't have kids, tried to distance me from my family, and made me feel I was a bad driver and therefore couldn't travel very far without him. I soon recognized these are some of the earmarks of an emotionally abusive relationship.

I also did some reading, and came across Bonnie Kaye's website. Her essay, "Perpetual Closet-Men," about men who spend a lifetime in denial, punishing and blaming their wives for their unhappiness rather than facing up to their true orientation, seemed to describe Yukio. I also found much support on the Straight Spouses Network website, the Yahoo! Wives of Bi/Gay Husbands support group, and at the website http://samvak.tripod.com/ (on dealing with narcissists). I took lessons in the Alexander Technique, a relaxation and movement practice that helped me reduce stress. I opened up to a few close friends about my marital confusion. I felt like I was slowly pulling myself up out of quicksand, and was relieved to find others willing to hold on to the other end of the rope.

During the summer, we tried couples therapy. Yukio denied being controlling, manipulative, or attracted to men. At first, he even attempted to deny he had made sexual advances to Hector and Raj. I was dismayed by the depth of his resistance, and he seemed to be shocked by what was coming out of my mouth. "I think she's the only person on earth who thinks I'm homosexual," he said at one session. Repeatedly, he tried to link his interest in gay porn to my alleged bad housekeeping.

The two therapists we saw said I needed to understand Yukio's position, his difficult childhood. And after all, if he was willing to have sex with me, didn't that prove he was straight? I attempted to explain, but failed to communicate to them my position: all these explanations, these positive things about Yukio, the traumas he experienced, these extenuating circumstances—these were all the same arguments I used on myself through the years to justify the relationship. And they weren't working anymore.

In the fall, I concluded the marriage had to end, but was delayed by practicalities: my daughter had just entered kindergarten and was still absorbing our move from a rural area to a busy suburb, and then, the day before Thanksgiving, my mother-in-law had a stroke.

Early in 2006, I saw a lawyer, and realized I needed to gather as much paperwork as I could, since I knew Yukio would probably hide everything once he knew I was divorcing him, and this prediction turned out to be accurate. It took me months, as I squeezed in work on the divorce while trying to maintain normal family and social life for my daughter.

Finally, in May, I filed for divorce and left my husband. The first couple of nights were agonizing. The relationship was like an addiction, and the transition was an enormous psychological shock. Deep down I still loved this man but was determined not to let him fill the rest of my life with his misery. In the weeks since then, my optimism and confidence have risen day by day, and I am amazed by how little I miss him. We are currently working through custody issues, and true to his controlling, narcissistic nature, he is trying to get a far greater share of our daughter's time than he had when we were all living under the same roof.

It is a typical story, and I know as I proceed through the next year, I will face many challenges in completing this divorce, in helping my daughter transition, and in returning to the work world. But now I can sleep again, I can digest my food again, and I no longer have to live in fear, in a shadow world of my husband's devising. I know I can handle things as long as I do what I have been doing since early 2005: taking one day at a time, seeking support and friendship, believing in myself, and being very sensitive to signals from my heart, brain, and gut to steer clear of those who would use my own impulses to imprison me.

Story 26 - Fully Awake Finally! By Jane A.

Married in a large wedding after dating seven years, I was not aware of anything unusual in our relationship. Love was in full bloom as we proceeded to get his law degree and I taught school. In the second year of our union, I became pregnant with our first child. Two years later we had another child, four years later another child, then nine years later another. There were subtle changes in our relationship, but I chose to believe what he said instead of my intuitions.

Having responsibilities for other little people's lives, working at various positions in education, running a home, church jobs, etc. were all my lot. He was a successful attorney in our home town. He was busy as well and soon we had two homes though on a very slim budget. He loved our boys and so did I. Life was a whirl of responsibilities and some enjoyment for me. I felt I could over give for a season expecting to see the fruit of my labors later.

What a mistake. He took on more work as I took over the home and family. He enjoyed male companionship more than his family. There were men of every age who became a limb off of our family. I would complain and he would return for a season.

He had become a workaholic as well as alcoholic. Whatever he did he overdid, but not concerning our family. Our children were all extremely well rounded, successful, and upstanding by the grace of God. They are all very successful, and I am very proud of them. I have four wonderful sons and eight wonderful grandchildren who make my 40 year marriage worthwhile. During those forty years, I tried everything I knew to do to make our relationship a solid one, ending up hopelessly existing and depressed. I went for counseling and took meds for five years as well as attended Alaon and Codependency sessions. I kept thinking if I could get it right our marriage would work—it didn't.

He was always over involved with other males. He was very proud of our sons' accomplishment in sports and academia but did not teach them out of his brilliance. He definitely preferred males other than his own children. I had not grown up with a father who was involved with my life other than to let me know what he expected of me. I allowed my mate to follow this pattern since it felt normal. There were tell tale signs that I questioned my husband about only to be told he was just trying to help the male involved.

In our forty-year marriage, I sought information concerning sexual arousals at inappropriate times (I thought) in the company of other males only to be given absolutely nothing definitive concerning this response—erections—which he laughingly denied as fact. My eyes were deceiving me. He, remember, is an attorney.

I merely supported us while he got his law degree. Having been born in an all girl family, I felt very inadequate around maleness and this added to my lack of understanding sexual responses among males. Eventually, after all our children were married, our third child began to walk into very clearly compromising places (hearing his father and a man talking in the bedroom of our home while I was away) early in the morning. His father admitted to a sexual relation to this son but begged for secrecy and promised to never be involved with the man again, only to be caught again a month and a half later by the same son. My son was 35 years old in a crumbling marriage with three precious children. By the grace of God, he is continuing to heal from this horrendous deception.

One of my sons is divorced and is living the homosexual lifestyle, but as he came out and adjusted to his new lifestyle, my ex husband had no real comfort for this child's anguish.

Who this creature is that I married is a real enigma. He is a liar, a deceiver, an adulterer, and worse than an animal since he has no integrity and lived a lie causing me and our children to live a lie. He only admitted to his homosexuality throughout our marriage, and before, after our sons attorneys themselves, questioned him for 8 hours in an intervention. Afterwards, I came in and heard him admit the same.

I am divorced and living a very peaceful life but I haven't been freed from the loss of a sexual relation, especially knowing he has a "glowing" one and enjoys what he committed to me and seems to think he is due it. Horrid man that he is, I do not want a relationship of any sort with him but I do feel anger to know that what I considered a sacred trust was just a sham and a pretense for the forty years we were married.

Story Number 27 - "Sunshine After The Storm" by Connie J

I met my ex through a friend who thought he was a nice guy, so I gave her permission to give him my phone number. He called me and we talked for hours. I thought he was the sweetest guy on earth. He said all the right things, he made me smile. A week later we went on our first date. Movies and dinner, we had a wonderful time. I even got my first kiss that night. We had dated for about three months when he asked me to move in with him. I did, and three months later we got married.

Things were great at first, we did everything together I guess you could say we were the perfect couple. He was so good to me in other ways it didn't really bother me about affection. But as the years went by and the children came along (3 sons currently ages 12, 10, and 9) things started to change.

I started to realize that I was being neglected sexually. I was the only one who always wanted it. When we did have sex it was like he was doing me a favor. He never wanted me to touch him anywhere. He never touched me it was just plain sex. I would ask him on several occasions why he didn't give me affection his response was "some men are not affectionate" and I started believing it. Maybe I had just married one of those men.

By our tenth year of marriage, our sex life was about over. I begged him for sex. He was always too tired. He would never go to bed when I went to bed he would stay up and watch television to avoid having sex with me.

In July of 2002, we went to Gulf Shores with a few other couples from our church. We had a room with double beds. He told me that he did not want to sleep in the bed with me. So for the entire trip of four days we slept in separate beds. This bothered me for a while. I asked him if he was angry with me, but he said no. He just didn't feel good during the trip and wanted to be left alone.

In August of 2002, I finally got up enough nerve to ask him was he gay. He went crazy. He started calling me names, telling me that I was not a good mother, nor a good wife, and that I was disgusting which is why he didn't want to have sex with me. It was all about me, I was the bad one. He denied he was gay. We stayed up to 5:00 a.m. that morning arguing. He moved in the guest room and remained there until I left which was October 2003.

I went through a living hell from August 2002 until October 2003. We lived as strangers, we were roommates. He didn't talk to me. He got a settlement for $26,000.00 and opened a separate account. He only gave me $200.00. He bought him a new car. Every weekend he would leave me and the boys and didn't even say where he was going. Things were so bad. I was very depressed and suicidal. I felt like I was doomed in this relationship for the rest of my life. I thought there was no way out.

I went to the doctor and he diagnosed me as being depressed and started me on medication. The medicine helped but the pain was still there. One day I got on the internet and went into history and found some of the websites he had been on—all gay websites. I even got into his email and read where he said he was gay and had been since he was 12 years old. He said in his email that he married me to make his mother happy and that the only way he could have sex with me was to think about a man doing him. This was devastating to me. I never told him that I had found out this information.

I went to the website about straight wives gay husbands and found Bonnie's website. I went there and viewed her books. I went and bought her book with the checklist on how you could know if your husband was gay. I contacted Bonnie and she sent me her autographed book Straight Wives/ Gay Husbands: A Mutation of Life. I read this book and it contained everything I was going through. Bonnie and her book gave me the inspiration to leave. I was so afraid, and I didn't know if I could make it financially.

In October 2003 I filed for divorce. One of my ex's friends worked in the courthouse and informed him that I had filed for divorce before he could receive his papers. He asked me had I filed for divorce and I said yes. He went crazy, called his family, and they all wanted to fight me. I had to call my sister and her husband to come and help me. I left with nothing. We lived on his family land and all his family was surrounded around us I was married to the whole family. I had to leave my children and all I had was the clothes I had on.

I contacted my lawyer and I had to get a police escort to get my clothes. He didn't let me see my children. We had to go to court and the court gave us equal time to have the children until the divorce.

I was scarred but happy that I was away from him. In January 2004 my mother passed away. She was my inspiration. She would call me everyday and tell me to hold my head up and things were going to be alright. I really almost lost my mind when she died. But I found out I was much stronger than I thought. We went to court three times. He had reported me to human services for child abuse to keep the children away from me. Every week the social workers were calling me about something. He had my children lying about things that didn't happen. It was awful. I went through a living hell. He tried to turn my children against me, but now the boys are fine. They have adjusted well.

I am presently in a wonderful relationship with a straight man. He is so loving and passionate. He makes me feel like a natural woman. I have my self and sexual esteem back. He gives me so much affection. Sometime I can't believe how happy I am, I think I'm dreaming. My children love him. I love him very much. We have been together 2 ½ years. We are planning on getting married sometime this year. I never thought I could leave my ex, but I did and I will never ever regret it. I am enjoying the sunshine after the storm.

My Conclusion – By Bonnie Kaye

I feel as if this book needs a conclusion. There are certain thoughts that should be spoken after reading these stories.

First, if you are a woman who is married to a gay man, you need to understand why this happens. So many women question why a gay man would marry a woman. Did he do this because he hated women? Did he do this to use her for a cover? Was the whole marriage a lie?

The truth is that almost all gay men who marry women love their wives when they marry them—at least on some level. They are not doing it to destroy your life, but rather to save theirs. Gay men are hoping against hope that if they love you hard enough or long enough, they won't be gay. They are hoping that if they can perform sex with a woman then there is a chance that they could be straight. And for some gay men, those feelings for men are suppressed as the marriage starts off successfully. It's just that eventually those nagging male attractions resurface and become so strong that they can't be denied.

The problem is that men who are living this Alice in Wonderland topsy-turvy situation find themselves falling deeper and deeper into a big hole that is increasingly more difficult to climb out of. They become fearful of losing the family, friends, and credibility that comes along with the marriage. Some men can never come to terms with who they are and will allow their wives to wallow in their unhappiness until death do they part. They justify that whatever they are doing for their wives is enough because of financial support. But it's not.

The longer you live a lie, the more difficult it becomes to be honest. Lying becomes a way of life. It is not an easy way of life because keeping track of lies is a full-time job in itself.

Next, you need to understand the answer to these questions: "Was there something I missed? How could I have not known? Why didn't I see the signs?"

The signs were easy to miss. We don't understand homosexuality. We were taught to believe that people who are gay are attracted to the same sex—not the opposite sex. **And even if we were aware that there may have been gay activity in the past, we thought it was over.** We were brought up in a generation that believed that "experimenting" was within the norm. "He tried it—he didn't like it—and so he's straight." This is a common misconception. And for those of us who believed that this "one moment in time" was a possibility, it gave us the extra challenge of trying to make sure that our men understood that we could love them enough to make them forget that little glitch in their past. Combine our lack of knowledge with our husbands' protesting much too much, and you'll have a better idea of how this confusion happens. We are idealists who believe that loving someone enough conquers all—even gay behavior.

Of all of the women I've worked with through the years, only a handful actually knew before they married. *And if they knew*, they also believed that marriage meant that a man was committed to his wife and "chose" to give up his homosexual life. Don't forget—a large number of religions and cultures keep reminding us that "homosexuality is a choice—and encourage men to 'choose' wisely." If men themselves "choose" to negate their homosexuality, who are we to say they are wrong?

Many of us are confused by the "SEX THING." Yes, in most cases there is sex—at least in the beginning. And in some cases, it's good or even great sex. When people are young, touch feels good, so it's easier to accept having sex with a woman. There are a certain percentage of gay men who can "perform" sex in their teens, twenties, thirties, and even forties and fifties. As the years go by, the percentages dwindle, but starting out, most gay husbands are able to get an erection and have an orgasm. What they choose to do before or in-between varies. Some men never kiss; others never touch; some go immediately to the shower afterwards and skip out on the intimacy part that develops from making love to someone and sharing in the afterglow.

People tell me that many couples who are straight don't maintain excellent sex lives through the years. It is not uncommon for sex to decline as the years go on. But there is a difference. Sexual relations with straight couples may decrease as life gets busier, schedules get more hectic, and illness sets in. But in spite of the obstacles that keep people apart, there is not the sexual emotional abuse thrown at the woman making her feel as she is the "abnormal" one. Women aren't made to feel as if making love is an "imposition" or that their sex drive is "abnormal." Straight men don't continually look for excuses why they won't have sex with their wives, and if they can't have sex, they are not looking to place the blame with their wives.

The sexual rejection by the majority of gay men strips away the sexual esteem of women. Sexual esteem plays a major role in having good self-esteem, because it reflects who we are as women. No woman wants to feel undesirable or that she has "abnormal" sexual needs. It makes her start doubting herself as a human being which affects many aspects of her day-to-day living.

I have found that women who thought they had "satisfactory" sex with their gay husbands had limited previous sexual experience. They thought sex was satisfactory because "it happened." They didn't have anything to compare it to. And many of them felt that because their husbands felt it was satisfactory, they too should feel the same way. It is mind over body, I guess.

Some women tell me they have intimacy with their gay husbands. To them, intimacy means laying side by side—with or without holding each other—and talking about "stuff." It is intimacy without sex most of the time. And some women have confessed to me that *this is actually better than the sex*. They don't mind **not** having sex. This makes me very sad because what they are really saying is that they never knew how wonderful making love with a straight man can be as far as being fulfilling, gratifying, and satisfying. Many of these women have had only one man in their sexual lives—their gay

BONNIE KAYE, M.Ed.

husbands. They have nothing to compare it to or judge it by. They just know that they don't mind *not having it.* After all, sex is not all it's cracked up to be, *right? Wrong.* Rather, having sex with someone who doesn't want to have sex with you is not all it's cracked up to be. Sex is the foundation for intimacy. Intimacy is the closeness a couple feels towards each other when the act of sex is not available, but the holding, hugging, kissing, lying together, and feeling loved is still there. Can a couple have intimacy without having had a healthy sex life? I say no—in almost all cases. Intimacy develops through touch, feel, trust, and desire. Without that, you may as well lay in bed next to a brother or a cousin. You can have a nice conversation with them too.

Some women are misled by the term "Bisexuality." When they learned that their husbands had attractions to men, it was easy to be fooled into thinking their husbands were bisexual. After all, they are married. They want a wife—they want a man. It's nothing personal—it's that "other side" of them that needs fulfillment. They claim it has nothing to do with you and that you shouldn't personalize it. I have been criticized by the network of men who call themselves "bisexual" for my refusal to allow them to live in that comfort zone. Having a wife shouldn't afford you that luxury. To me, if a man is truly "bisexual," he should feel sexually satisfied with his wife and not have the need to act on sexual desires with men. The men who argue this with me the most often are men who have limited sexual encounters with their wives, but feel no regret about acting on their gay sexual impulses. They hide behind the security of a wife and family leading the "straight" life. Their wives never felt that passion from them that their gay lovers feel. This means they are emotionally straight but sexually gay. They desire men sexually. This is the cross over point to me. Once you act on your homosexual desires, you have crossed the border line into "gaydom." Learn to accept it and stop making excuses for it.

I tell my women that it doesn't matter what a man wants to call himself. If he desires or acts on having sexual relations with

192

a man, he is gay. Period. He can be a gay husband, but he is gay and a husband. Don't get hung up on labels—get hung up on the action itself. Sometimes a woman feels better saying the word "Bisexual" because it gives her a false sense of hope. It makes her feel as if there is still a chance that the apple will fall on her side of the fence so to speak. Where there's Bi, there's hope. This is not the case. It is a false sense of security that will come crashing down one day. Learn to accept it, then move on and reject him. It is not a healthy way for any woman to have to live.

People tell me they stay together because of the children. Ouch. That one hurts. In this day and age, you would think they would have wised up. Staying for the sake of the children when you are unhappy in a marriage Is not doing them or you a favor. If you are unhappy in the marriage, don't you think your children know it? They do—and they blame themselves because they see you are staying in an unhappy relationship due to them. They are standing n your way of being happy. And here's another important point. Remember the old "monkey see, monkey do, money act just like you" rhyme? Well, that simple little phrase holds a whole lot of meaning. If your children see that you are unhappy, they will accept this is how marriage is supposed to be when they grow up and find themselves in a similar predicament. We need to be role models to our children and show them that we are strong in the face of adversity and not willing to give in to destructive patterns that shave years off our emotional well-being. You saw this stated in some of the stories you just read. Let them give you the courage to start moving away from the drama and the trauma.

Recovery from marriage to a gay husband takes time. All women who go through divorce go through some of the same problems, such as single parenthood, financial problems, selling the home and moving, and legal tangles that can put you into or near bankruptcy. But in addition, we are forced to deal with a set of additional issues that are unique and unlike those that women with straight husbands face. We have to figure out what to say to the children and when to tell them. We also have to decide what to tell family, friends, and co-workers. We live in a world where people still don't understand about a gay husband and fear the ridicule we will face from them. There are many ignorant people out there. Even in this day and age, people say, "What did you do to make him gay? After all, he wasn't gay when he married you."

We have to rebuild our own self-esteem, which has been sorely damaged through these marriages by not only feeling the failure of a marriage, but also wondering how much of a lie we were living. We have to rebuild our sense of trust within our own decision-making processes knowing that we walked blindly into a situation where we were so misled. Most of us have lost or never had the feeling of what real intimacy means in a relationship. We have difficulty trusting men again and trusting our own ability not to walk into this situation one more time. And this is a genuine fear that many women express—"It happened to me once. How do I know the next man I get involved with won't be gay?" After all, why couldn't we tell the first time around? This is confirmed by the ignorance of others who insist that we "must have known but married him anyway because we thought we could change him."

There are other complications as well. There are those women who still feel some sense of responsibility for their husbands' homosexuality. They are convinced that they played some part in their husbands turning to men. That's because some gay husbands are cruel enough to say that to them rather than take the responsibility for the truth.

We have to deal with our own feelings of homophobia. Even if we are understanding of homosexuality in general terms, "gay" takes on a whole new meaning when it enters our marriages and ruins our hopes and dreams for our futures with our husbands.

We have to face the reality of seeing the man we love with a man he loves when our husbands bring their new lovers into the lives of our children. We worry about how that will affect our children emotionally. We have to fear how other people will treat our children if they find out they have a gay father. And of course, we now have to contend with the possibility that our children will be gay because this is a new reality we didn't think of before. Statistically, there is more of chance that a gay parent will have a gay child. This is something you must be mentally prepared for, and not let your own disappointment with your husband over cloud your feelings if this should happen to one of your children. Homosexuality is not a choice—it's genetic. The last thing you want for your child is for him or her to grow up thinking that something is wrong with homosexuality, forcing him or her to jump into the same closet as your husband is or was locked in.

For these reasons, ***Gay Husband Recovery*** takes time. Sometimes it takes a lot of time depending on how your husband handles it. If he is responsible and takes care of his family, it helps to ease the readjustment. If he is irresponsible and selfish, the anger takes longer to move past. Eventually things will equal out because time is a great healer, but some scars are bound to remain. And that's okay. We are not machines that can just wipe away the emotional impact, nor should anyone tell you how you should feel after this disaster.

The most important lesson to be learned from this book is that gay husbands come in all varieties. There is no one type although there is a prototype. Some of these men have sex; some don't. Some are your best friends; others aren't. Some are nice guys, some are sociopaths. Some are submissive; others are controlling. Some tell the truth eventually; some never do or never will. It would be so much easier if there was just a simple way to tell—but there's not.

Some women will never have confirmation about their suspicions. That's why so many languish for years in these unfulfilling relationships—THEY HAVE NO PROOF. I'm never quite clear why women feel they need "proof." Living in an unfulfilling relationship should be enough of a reason to get out of it. The only proof you should need is that you are unhappy.

I understand how difficult it is to end a marriage, no matter how unhappy you are. I never sit here and say, "If I can do it, you can do it." That would be cold and insensitive on my part. What I do say is that if you want to do it, someday it will hopefully happen, but it may take some time. The important thing is to keep sight of what the goal is. The goal is to take back whatever good years you keep losing and to find happiness within yourself again. You don't have to find the love of your life; you just have to start to love your life and be free of the pain. Many women write to say that they wish they could meet a wonderful man who will be their partner in life. But you can only meet someone who is your true love after you relearn to re-love and trust yourself again. Then it will fall into place.

No woman is an island. We all need help and support. Living with a gay man is isolating enough because we live our lives as detectives, waiting to trap him. And then when we catch him, we think we need more evidence and want to catch him again. That's because every time he's caught, he denies your evidence, waters it down to being some kind of "curiosity" moment, or promises it will never, ever, happen again. *Right.*

Well, actually, I meant to say *"wrong."* Your gay husband **will not change**. You can wish for it, pray for it, or go for counseling for it, but it is *not happening*. He might try in earnest and be sincere when he says it won't happen again, but he's fooling himself—and you. Gay is not a choice—it is a state of being. People can control their behavior, but they have no control over their sexuality. What does this mean? It means that your husbands have **no choice** in being gay—but they have a choice on acting on it and on being honest with you.

Some women believe that their husbands love them and their marriages enough to deeply bury their homosexuality. And, some men really do make the effort. But guess what? They are not happy campers. They love you, but you can't fulfill the need they have within them either emotionally or physically. I believe that they have a mental need to be in their marriage, but their thoughts and hearts are always somewhere else. They are gay.

You are a woman. You can't give them what they want aside from being a security blanket.

Some gay men can have sex with their wives. **They still want a man**. A few gay men can even satisfy a woman. **They still want a man**. A few RARE women have told me that their husbands were great in bed. I believe their husbands were great actors. One gay husband recently wrote to me that he has spent years studying how to satisfy a woman because he loves his wife to make sure she is satisfied. But—**he still wants a man**. She is satisfied—he isn't.

When a man isn't happy with his life, he's not happy with his life **with you**. He may love you, but either consciously or unconsciously, he starts to believe that **you** are the obstacle standing in the way between him and happiness. And so he looks to find fault with you because it's easier than accepting responsibility for it himself. Once again, this isn't about love—it's about sexuality. And sexuality isn't always just about sex—it's about the things that go with sex like intimacy—something that he wants from the same person he wants to have sex with—*which isn't you.*

I want to end this book with feelings of hope. You can see that women do go on to new relationships and marriages. Some of them do live happily ever re-after. Other women learn to love themselves enough to find fulfillment being on their own. I was once one of those women. After my divorce from my gay husband many years ago, I spent 11 years building myself up and repairing my heavily damaged ego. I raised two little kids, went to college, earned a Master's Degree, went to work, started counseling and writing. I had friends and family surrounding me, and I was happy without a man. I didn't need a man to make me feel complete. I was complete. And it was only once I understood that I was the master of my own happiness that I allowed my heart to open up and try again. I found a man who could make me feel alive again as a sexual woman. He learned to meet my emotional needs, and we have spun our own world into a beautiful dream.

If any of you are left standing on the fence after reading the accounts from these wonderful brave women, please jump over it and begin taking back your life. You are not alone—there is plenty of support out there. And I am here for you.

—Bonnie Kaye, M.Ed.

www.Gayhusbands.com

CPSIA information can be obtained
at www.ICGtesting.com
Printed in the USA
BVHW081133050221
599218BV00001B/33